THE
PASSION
TRANSLATION

2020
edition

THE BOOK OF

PROVERBS

wisdom from above

BroadStreet
PUBLISHING

The Passion Translation®
Proverbs: Wisdom from Above

Published by BroadStreet Publishing® Group, LLC
BroadStreetPublishing.com
ThePassionTranslation.com

The Passion Translation is a registered trademark of Passion & Fire Ministries, Inc.

Copyright © 2017, 2018, 2020 Passion & Fire Ministries, Inc.

For information about bulk sales or customized editions of The Passion Translation, please contact orders@broadstreetpublishing.com.

The publisher and TPT team have worked diligently and prayerfully to present this version of The Passion Translation Bible with excellence and accuracy. If you find a mistake in the Bible text or footnotes, please contact the publisher at tpt@broadstreetpublishing.com.

978-1-4245-6342-5 (paperback)
978-1-4245-6343-2 (e-book)

Printed in the United States of America

21 22 23 24 25 5 4 3 2 1

A NOTE TO READERS

It would be impossible to calculate how many lives have been changed forever by the power of the Bible, the living Word of God! My own life was transformed because I believed the message contained in Scripture about Jesus, the Savior.

To hold the Bible dear to your heart is the sacred obsession of every true follower of Jesus. Yet to go even further and truly understand the Bible is how we gain light and truth to live by. Did you catch the word *understand*? People everywhere say the same thing: "I want to understand God's Word, not just read it."

Thankfully, as English speakers, we have a plethora of Bible translations, commentaries, study guides, devotionals, churches, and Bible teachers to assist us. Our hearts crave to know God—to not just know about him, but to know him as intimately as we possibly can in this life. This is what makes Bible translations so valuable, because each one will hopefully lead us into new discoveries of God's character. I believe God is committed to giving us truth in a package we can understand and apply, so I thank God for every translation of God's Word that we have.

God's Word does not change, but over time languages definitely do, thus the need for updated and revised translations of the Bible. Translations give us the words God spoke through his servants, but words can be poor containers for revelation because they leak! Meaning is influenced by culture, background, and many other details. Just imagine how differently the Hebrew authors of the Old Testament saw the world three thousand years ago from the way we see it today!

Even within one language and culture, meanings of words change from one generation to the next. For example, many contemporary Bible readers would be quite surprised to find unicorns are mentioned nine times in the King James Version (KJV). Here's one instance in Isaiah 34:7: "And the unicorns shall come down with them, and the bullocks with the bulls; and their land shall be soaked with blood, and their dust made fat with fatness." This isn't a result of poor translation, but rather an example of how our culture, language, and understanding of the world has shifted over the past few centuries. So, it is important that we have a modern English text of the Bible that releases revelation and truth into our hearts. The Passion Translation (TPT) is committed to bringing forth the potency of God's Word in relevant, contemporary vocabulary that doesn't distract from its meaning or distort it in any way. So many people have told us that they are falling in love with the Bible again as they read TPT.

We often hear the statement, "I just want a word-for-word translation that doesn't mess it up or insert a bias." That's a noble desire. But a word-for-word translation would be nearly unreadable. It is simply impossible to translate one Hebrew word for one English word. Hebrew is built from triliteral consonant roots. Biblical Hebrew had no vowels or punctuation. And Koine Greek, although wonderfully articulate, cannot always be conveyed in English by a word-for-word translation. For example, a literal word-for-word translation of the Greek in Matthew 1:18 would be something like this: "Of the but Jesus Christ the birth thus was. Being betrothed the mother of him, Mary, to

Joseph, before or to come together them she was found in belly having from Spirit Holy."

Even the KJV, which many believe to be a very literal translation, renders this verse: "Now the birth of Jesus Christ was on this wise: When as his mother Mary was espoused to Joseph, before they came together, she was found with child of the Holy Ghost."

This comparison makes the KJV look like a paraphrase next to a strictly literal translation! To some degree, every Bible translator is forced to move words around in a sentence to convey with meaning the thought of the verse. There is no such thing as a truly literal translation of the Bible, for there is not an equivalent language that perfectly conveys the meaning of the biblical text. Is it really possible to have a highly accurate and highly readable English Bible? We certainly hope so! It is so important that God's Word is living in our hearts, ringing in our ears, and burning in our souls. Transferring God's revelation from Hebrew and Greek into English is an art, not merely a linguistic science. Thus, we need all the accurate translations we can find. If a verse or passage in one translation seems confusing, it is good to do a side-by-side comparison with another version.

It is difficult to say which translation is the "best." "Best" is often in the eyes of the reader and is determined by how important differing factors are to different people. However, the "best" translation, in my thinking, is the one that makes the Word of God clear and accurate, no matter how many words it takes to express it.

That's the aim of The Passion Translation: to bring God's eternal truth into a highly readable heart-level expression that causes truth and love to jump out of the text and lodge inside our hearts. A desire to remain accurate to the text and a desire to communicate God's heart of passion for his people are the two driving forces behind TPT. So for those new to Bible reading, we hope TPT will excite and illuminate. For scholars and Bible students, we hope TPT will bring the joys of new discoveries from the text and prompt deeper consideration of what God has spoken to his people. We all have so much more to learn and discover about God in his holy Word!

You will notice at times we've italicized certain words or phrases. These portions are not in the original Hebrew, Greek, or Aramaic manuscripts but are implied from the context. We've made these implications explicit for the sake of narrative clarity and to better convey the meaning of God's Word. This is a common practice by mainstream translations.

We've also chosen to translate certain names in their original Hebrew or Greek forms to better convey their cultural meaning and significance. For instance, some translations of the Bible have substituted James for Jacob and Jude for Judah. Both Greek and Aramaic manuscripts leave these Hebrew names in their original forms. Therefore, this translation uses those cultural names.

The purpose of The Passion Translation is to reintroduce the passion and fire of the Bible to the English reader. It doesn't merely convey the literal meaning of words. It expresses God's passion for people and his world by translating the original, life-changing message of God's Word for modern readers.

We pray this version of God's Word will kindle in you a burning desire to know the heart of God, while impacting the church for years to come.

Please visit **ThePassionTranslation.com** for more information.

Brian Simmons and the translation team

PROVERBS

Introduction

ABOUT PROVERBS

The Bible is a book of poetry, not simply starched, stiff doctrines devoid of passion. The Bible, including Proverbs, is full of poetic beauty and subtle nuances ripe with meaning. The ancient wisdom of God fills its pages!

Proverbs is a book of wisdom from above tucked inside metaphors, symbols, and poetic imagery. God could

properly be described as the divine poet and master arti-
san who crafted the cosmos to portray his glory and has
given us his written Word to reveal his wisdom. Inspired
from eternity, the sixty-six books of our Bible convey the
full counsel and wisdom of God. Do you need wisdom?
God has a verse for that!

Five books of divine poetry show us the reality of
knowing God through experience, not just through his-
tory or doctrines. Job points us to the end of our self-life
to discover the greatest revelation of the Lord, which is
his tender love and wisdom. Psalms reveals the new life
we enter into with God, expressed through praise and
prayer. Next is Proverbs, where we enroll in the divine
seminary of wisdom and revelation to learn the ways of
God. Ecclesiastes teaches us to set our hearts not on the
things of this life but on those values that endure eter-
nally. And finally, in Song of Songs, the sweetest lyrics
ever composed lead us into divine romance where we are
immersed in Jesus' love for his bride.

The nature of Hebrew poetry is quite different from that
of English poetry. There is a pleasure found in Hebrew
poetry that transcends rhyme and meter. The Hebrew
verses come in a poetic package, a form of meaning that
imparts an understanding that is deeper than mere logic.
True revelation unfolds an encounter—an experience of
knowing God as he is revealed through the mysterious
vocabulary of riddle, proverb, and parable.

For example, the Hebrew word for "proverb," *mashal*,
has two meanings. The first is "parable, byword, metaphor, a pithy saying that expresses wisdom." But the
second meaning is overlooked by many. The homonym
mashal can also mean "to rule, to take dominion" or "to
reign with power."

What you have before you now is a dynamic translation
of the ancient book of Proverbs. These powerful words

will bring you revelation from the throne room—the wisdom you need to guide your steps and direct your life. What you learn from these verses will change your life and launch you into your destiny.

PURPOSE

Within this divinely anointed compilation of proverbs there is a deep well of wisdom to reign in our lives and to succeed in our destiny. The wisdom that God has designed for us to receive will cause us to excel—to rise up as rulers-to-be on earth for his glory. The kingdom of God is brought into the earth as we implement the godly wisdom of Proverbs.

Although the book of Proverbs can be interpreted in its most literal and practical sense, the wisdom contained herein is not unlocked by a casual surface reading. The Spirit of revelation has breathed upon every verse to embed a deeper meaning of practical insight to guide our steps into the lives God meant for us to live.

AUTHOR AND AUDIENCE

You're about to read the greatest book of wisdom ever written, mostly penned by the wisest man to ever live. God gave Solomon this wisdom to pass along to us, God's servants, who continue the ministry of Jesus, the embodiment of wisdom, until he returns in full glory. While Solomon penned most of these words of wisdom, it is believed others had a hand too, including advisers to King Hezekiah and the unknown men Agur and Lemuel—which could be pseudonyms for Solomon. Regardless, the one who edited the final version of Proverbs brought together the wisest teachings from the wisest person to ever live to write a book containing some of the deepest revelation in the Bible. When Solomon pens a proverb, there is more than meets the eye!

To whom are these proverbs written? This compilation of wisdom's words is written to you! Throughout the book we find words like "Listen, my sons. Listen, my daughters." The book of Proverbs is written to us as sons and daughters of the living God. The teaching we receive is not from a distant god who tells us we'd better live right or else. These are personal words of love and tenderness from our wise Father, the Father of eternity, who speaks right into our hearts with healing, radiant words. Receive deeply the words of the kind Father of heaven as though he were speaking directly to you.

MAJOR THEMES

The wisdom found in Proverbs is about the art of successful living. The appeal of these insights is that they touch on universal problems and issues that affect human behavior in us all. Several major themes are present in these godly sayings of God's servant Solomon:

Lady Wisdom, Revelation-Knowledge, Living-Understanding. Throughout Proverbs wisdom is personified with the metaphor of Lady Wisdom, who dispenses revelation-knowledge and living-understanding. Lady Wisdom is a figure of speech for God, whose divine wisdom invites us to receive the best way to live, the excellent and noble way of life. Wisdom is personified as a guide (6:22), a beloved sister or bride (7:4), and a hostess who generously invites people to "come and dine at my table and drink of my wine" (9:1–6). In Proverbs, wisdom is inseparable from knowledge and understanding, which is not received independent of God's revelation. We are invited to "come to the one who has living-understanding" (9:10) in order to receive what Lady Wisdom has to offer. God promises that revelation-knowledge will flow to the one who hungers for the gift of understanding (14:6).

The Fear of the Lord. From the beginning, in 1:7, Proverbs makes it clear that we "gain the essence of wisdom" and "cross the threshold of true knowledge" only when we fear the Lord—or, as The Passion Translation reads, we live "in obedient devotion to God." Living in a way that our entire being worships and adores God is a constant theme throughout Proverbs.

God's Transcendence and Immanence. Proverbs teaches that God is both the author of (transcendent) and actor within (immanent) our human story. First, God is above and outside the world: as Creator "he broke open the hidden fountains of the deep, bringing secret springs to the surface" (3:20); "God sees everything you do and his eyes are wide open as he observes every single habit you have" (5:21); he is sovereign and steers "a king's heart for his purposes" as easily as he directs "the course of a stream" (21:1).

Second, God is a part of and involved with the world: "The rich and the poor have one thing in common: the Lord God created each one" (22:2); "the Lord champions the widow's cause" (15:25); he "will rise to plead [the poor's] case" (22:23).

Proverbs teaches that God is all-powerful and transcendent while also taking part in our human story as our defender and protector.

Wise and Fool, Righteous and Wicked. Solomon believed there are basically two kinds of people in the world: the wise righteous and the wicked fools. The wise person possesses God's revelation-knowledge and living-understanding. Therefore, he is prudent, shrewd, insightful, and does what is right because he is righteous, a God-lover. This lover of God is just, peaceful, upright, blameless, good, trustworthy, and kind.

The wicked fool is different. He is greedy, violent, deceitful, cruel, and he speaks perversely. It's no wonder "the Lord detests the lifestyle of the wicked" (15:9)! As a foolish person, he is described as being gullible, an idiot, self-sufficient, a mocker, lazy, senseless, and one who rejects revelation-knowledge and living-understanding.

Many of Solomon's wise sayings relate to these two kinds of people, teaching us how to avoid being a wicked fool and instead live as God intends us to live, as his wise, righteous lovers.

Wealth and Poverty. As with many of Solomon's wise sayings, we cannot take one thought on wealth and poverty and apply it to every situation. Instead, Solomon teaches us seven major things about having wealth and being poor, and how wisdom and foolishness affect them both: the righteous are blessed with wealth by God himself; foolishness leads to poverty; fools who have wealth will soon lose it; poverty results from injustice and oppression; the wealthy are called to be generous with their wealth; gaining wisdom is far better than gaining wealth; and the value of wealth is limited.

Jesus and the Church. As with the rest of the Old Testament, we are called to read Proverbs in light of Jesus and his ministry. Throughout the gospels Jesus associates himself with wisdom. For instance, in Matt. 11:18–19 Jesus claims his actions represent Lady Wisdom herself. Where he is identified with Lady Wisdom in the New Testament, it is a powerful way of saying that Jesus is the full, entire embodiment of wisdom. In many ways Col. 1:15–17 mirrors Prov. 8. Likewise, the preface to John's Gospel resonates with this same chapter when Jesus is associated with the Word, another personification of wisdom.

Jesus stands at the center of Scripture; he can be found throughout Scripture, not just in the New Testament. So as you read these important words of wisdom, consider how they point to the One who perfectly embodied and is our Wisdom.

PROVERBS

Wisdom from Above

The Prologue

1 Here are kingdom revelations, words to live by,
and words of wisdom given to empower you to
reign in life,[a]
written as proverbs by Israel's King Solomon,[b]
David's son.
[2] Within these sayings will be found the revelation of
wisdom[c]
and the impartation of spiritual understanding.
Use them as keys to unlock the treasures of true
knowledge.

---

a 1:1 As stated in the introduction, the Hebrew word for "proverbs"
means more than just a wise saying. It can also mean "to rule, to
reign in power, to take dominion."

b 1:1 The name Solomon means "peaceable." There is a greater one
than Solomon who gives peace to all of his followers. His name is
Jesus. Solomon was the seed of David; we are the seed of Jesus
Christ. Solomon had an encounter with God after asking for a discerning heart (1 Kings 3:5–14). This pleased God, so he gave Solomon wisdom, riches, and power. God is ready to impart these same
things today to those who ask him. See James 1:5–8.

c 1:2 There are six Hebrew words translated "wisdom" in the book of
Proverbs. Some of them require an entire phrase in English to convey the meaning. The word used here is *chokmah*, and it is used in
Proverbs forty-two times. Forty-two is the number of months Jesus
ministered and the number of generations from Abraham to Christ
listed in Matt. 1.

³Those who cling to these words will receive discipline
  to demonstrate wisdom[a] in every relationship
  and to choose what is right and just and fair.
⁴These proverbs will give you great skill
  to teach the immature and make them wise,
  to give youth the understanding of their design and
    destiny.
⁵For the wise, these proverbs will make you even
    wiser,
  and for those with discernment,
  you will be able to acquire brilliant strategies for
    leadership.
⁶These kingdom revelations will break open your
    understanding
  to unveil the deeper meaning of parables,
  poetic riddles, and epigrams,
  and to unravel the words and enigmas of the wise.
⁷We cross the threshold of true knowledge
  when we live in obedient devotion to God.[b]
  Stubborn know-it-alls[c] will never stop to do this,
  for they scorn true wisdom and knowledge.

---

a 1:3 The Hebrew word translated "wisdom" here also means "righteousness."

b 1:7 Many translations render this "the fear of the Lord." This means much more than the English concept of fear. It also implies submission, awe, worship, and reverence. The Hebrew word used here is found fourteen times in Proverbs. The number fourteen represents spiritual perfection. The number fourteen is mentioned three times in the genealogy of Jesus (Matt. 1:1–17). It is also the number for Passover. You will pass from darkness to wisdom's light by the "fear" of the Lord.

c 1:7 Or "foolish ones." There are three Hebrew words translated "fool" in Proverbs and another six that are related to a fool or foolish acts. A fool is described in Proverbs as one who hates true wisdom and correction, with no desire to acquire revelation knowledge.

The Wisdom of a Father

⁸Pay close attention, my child, to your father's wise
   words
   and never forget your mother's instructions.^a
⁹For their insight will bring you success,
   adorning you with grace-filled thoughts
   and giving you reins to guide your decisions.^b
¹⁰When peer pressure compels you to go with the
   crowd
   and sinners invite you to join in,
   you must simply say, "No!"
¹¹When the gang says—
   "We're going to steal and kill and get away with it.
¹²We'll take down the rich and rob them.
   We'll swallow them up alive
   and take what we want from whomever we want.
¹³Then we'll take their treasures and fill our homes
   with loot.
¹⁴So come on and join us.
   Take your chance with us.
   We'll divide up all we get;
   we'll each end up with big bags of cash!"—
¹⁵my son, refuse to go with them and stay far away
   from them.
¹⁶For crime is their way of life and bloodshed their
   specialty.

---

a 1:8 Many expositors see this verse as the words of David to Solomon, yet we all must give heed to this command. The words of our Father (God) and our mother (the church, the freewoman) will bring us wisdom. See Gal. 4:21–31.

b 1:9 The Hebrew text here is literally translated "adornment for your head, chains for your neck." The head is a metaphor for our thoughts, the neck a symbol for willing obedience that guides our decisions, in contrast to being stiff-necked or proud. See Phil. 2:5–7.

¹⁷To be aware of their snare is the best way of escape.
¹⁸They'll resort to murder to steal their victim's assets,
   but eventually it will be their own lives that are
      ambushed.
¹⁹In their ungodly disrespect for God
   they bring destruction on their own lives.

Wisdom's Warning

²⁰Wisdom's praises are sung in the streets
   and celebrated far and wide.
²¹Yet wisdom's song is not always heard in the halls of
   higher learning.
   But in the hustle and bustle of everyday life
   its lyrics can always be heard above the din of the
      crowd.ᵃ
   You will hear wisdom's warning as she preaches
      courageously
   to those who stop to listen:
²²"Foolish ones, how much longer will you cling to
   your deception?ᵇ
   How much longer will you mock wisdom,
   you cynical scorners who fight the facts?
²³Come back to your senses and be restored to reality.
   Don't even think about refusing my rebuke!
   Don't you know that I'm ready
   to pour out my spirit of wisdom upon you
   and bring to you the revelation of my words
   that will make your heart wise?

---

a 1:21 Literally translated, this verse reads "Wisdom sings out in the streets and speaks her voice in the squares, crying out at the head of noisy crowds and at the entrance of the city gates." This is a parabolic statement of wisdom being heard everywhere and in every place.

b 1:22 Or "Childish ones, how long will you love your childishness?"

²⁴I've called to you over and over;
   still you refuse to come to me.
   I've pleaded with you again and again,
   yet you've turned a deaf ear to my voice.
²⁵Because you have laughed at my counsel
   and have insisted on continuing in your
      stubbornness,
²⁶I will laugh when your calamity comes
   and will turn away from you at the time of your
      disaster.
   Make a joke of my advice, will you?
   Then I'll make a joke out of you!
²⁷When the storm clouds of terror gather over your
      head,
   when dread and distress consume you
   and your catastrophe comes like a hurricane,
²⁸you will cry out to me, but I won't answer.
   Then it will be too late to expect my help.
   When desperation drives you to search for me,
   I will be nowhere to be found.
²⁹Because you have turned up your nose at me
   and closed your eyes to the facts
   and refused to worship me in awe^a—
³⁰because you scoffed at my wise counsel
   and laughed at my correction—
³¹now you will eat the bitter fruit of your own ways.
   You've made your own bed; now lie in it!
   So how do you like that?
³²Like an idiot you've turned away from me
   and chosen destruction instead.

---

a 1:29 The Hebrew word used here can be translated "fear," "dread," "awe," or "worship." Nearly every translation uses the word *fear* or *reverence* while ignoring the other aspects of the Aramaic word *dekhlatha*. The New Testament is clear that there is no fear in love. See 1 John 4:18.

Your self-satisfied smugness[a] will kill you.
³³But the one who always listens to me
will live undisturbed in a heavenly peace.
Free from fear, confident and courageous,
that one will rest unafraid and sheltered from the
storms of life."

Searching for Wisdom

2 My child, will you treasure my wisdom?
Then, and only then, will you acquire it.
And only if you accept my advice
and hide it within will you succeed.
²So train your heart to listen when I speak
and open your spirit wide to expand your
discernment—
then pass it on to your sons and daughters.[b]
³Yes, cry out for comprehension and intercede for insight.
⁴For if you keep seeking it like a man would seek for
sterling silver,
searching in hidden places for cherished treasure,
⁵then you will discover the fear of the Lord
and find the true knowledge of God.
⁶Wisdom is a gift from a generous God,
and every word he speaks is full of revelation
and becomes a fountain of understanding within you.[c]
⁷⁻⁸For the Lord has a hidden storehouse of wisdom
made accessible to his godly ones.[d]
He becomes your personal bodyguard as you follow
his ways,
protecting and guarding you as you choose what is
right.

---

a 1:32 Or "your abundant prosperity."
b 2:2 As translated from the Septuagint.
c 2:6 The Septuagint adds "found in his presence."
d 2:7–8 Or "the righteous."

⁹Then you will discover all that is just, proper, and fair,
   and be empowered to make the right decisions
   as you walk into your destiny.
¹⁰When wisdom wins your heart and revelation breaks in,
   true pleasure enters your soul.
¹¹If you choose to follow good counsel,
   divine design will watch over you
   and understanding will protect you
   from making poor choices.
¹²It will rescue you from evil in disguise
   and from those who speak duplicities.
¹³For they have left the paths of righteousness
   and walk in the ways of darkness.
¹⁴They take pleasure when evil prospers
   and thoroughly enjoy a lifestyle of sin.
¹⁵But they're walking on a path to nowhere,
   wandering away into deeper deception.

Wisdom, the Way of the Pure

¹⁶Only wisdom can save you from the flattery
   of the promiscuous woman—
   she's such a smooth-talking seductress!
¹⁷She left her husband and has forgotten her wedding vows.[a]

---

a 2:17 Clearly this is a warning to those who would commit adultery, but there is a deeper meaning within this text. Proverbs tells us of two women: the adulteress and the virtuous woman of Prov. 31. Both women speak a parable of two systems in the church. One is religious and alluring, tempting the young anointed ones to come to her "bed" of compromise (see Mark 7:13). The other is the holy bride, virtuous and pure, keeping her first love ("wedding vows") for Christ alone. Her "house" is the house of the Lord (see Prov. 2:18). One system brings shame and despair; the other brings favor, honor, and glory. It is wisdom that protects us from one and unites us to the other. See Jer. 50–52 and Rev. 17–18.

¹⁸You'll find her house on the road to hell,
¹⁹and all the men who go through her doors
    will never come back to the place they were—
    they will find nothing but desolation and despair.
²⁰Follow those who follow wisdom and stay on the
    right path.
²¹For all my godly lovers will enjoy life to the fullest
    and will inherit their destinies.ᵃ
²²But the treacherous ones who love darkness
    will lose not only all they could have had,
    but even their own souls!

The Rewards of Wisdom

3 ¹⁻²My child, if you truly want a long and satisfying
    life,
    never forget the things that I've taught you.
    Follow closely every truth that I've given you.
    Then you will have a full, rewarding life.
³Hold on to loyal love and don't let go,
    and be faithful to all that you've been taught.
    Let your life be shaped by integrity,ᵇ
    with truth written upon your heart.
⁴That's how you will find favor and understanding
    with both God and men—
    you will gain the reputation of living life well.

Wisdom's Guidance

⁵Trust in the Lord completely,
    and do not rely on your own opinions.
    With all your heart rely on him to guide you,
    and he will lead you in every decision you make.

---

a 2:21 Literally "shall dwell in the land."
b 3:3 Or "Tie my commands around your neck." The neck is a symbol
    of our will and conscience.

⁶Become intimate with him in whatever you do,
    and he will lead you wherever you go.ᵃ
⁷Don't think for a moment that you know it all,ᵇ
    for wisdom comes when you adore him with undi-
        vided devotion
    and avoid everything that's wrong.
⁸Then you will find the healing refreshment
    your body and spirit long for.ᶜ
⁹Glorify God with all your wealth,
    honoring him with your firstfruits,
    with every increase that comes to you.
¹⁰Then every dimension of your life will overflow with
    blessings
    from an uncontainable source of inner joy!

Wisdom's Correction
¹¹My child, when the Lord God speaks to you,
    never take his words lightly,
    and never be upset when he corrects you.
¹²For the Father's discipline comes only
    from his passionate love and pleasure for you.
    Even when it seems like his correction is harsh,
    it's still better than any father on earth gives to his
        child.
¹³Blessings pour over the ones who find wisdom,
    for they have obtained living-understanding.ᵈ

---

a 3:6 Or "he will cut a straight path before you."
b 3:7 We should always be willing to listen to correction and instruction.
c 3:8 Literally "healing to your navel and moistening to your bones." The blood supply for a baby in the womb comes through the navel. New cells are made in the marrow of our bones. As the navel and bones picture the life flow of our bodies, so the navel and bones are a picture of our inner being. See John 7:37–39.
d 3:13 The Hebrew text here implies that wisdom gives the ability to take raw facts and draw right conclusions and meaning from them.

¹⁴As wisdom increases, a great treasure is imparted,
   greater than many bars of refined gold.
¹⁵It is a more valuable commodity than gold and
   gemstones,^a
   for there is nothing you desire that could compare
      to her.
¹⁶Wisdom extends to you long life in one hand
   and wealth and promotion^b in the other.
   Out of her mouth flows righteousness,
   and her words release both law and mercy.^c
¹⁷The ways of wisdom are sweet,
   always drawing you into the place of wholeness.^d
¹⁸Seeking for her brings the discovery of untold
   blessings,
   for she is the healing tree of life to those who taste
      her fruits.^e

Wisdom's Blueprints

¹⁹The Lord laid the earth's foundations with wisdom's
   blueprints.
   By his living-understanding all the universe came
      into being.^f

---

a 3:15 The Hebrew word translated here as "gemstones" can also refer
to rubies, coral, or pearls.
b 3:16 Or "honor."
c 3:16 The Septuagint adds this last sentence, which is not found in
the Hebrew.
d 3:17 The Hebrew word translated here as "wholeness" can also
mean "peace" or "prosperity."
e 3:18 Verses 17 and 18 are recited in contemporary Torah services as
the Torah scroll is returned to the ark, where it is kept.
f 3:19 When compared with Col. 1:16, we can see that Wisdom is used
as a title in Proverbs for the Living Wisdom, Jesus Christ. See 1 Cor.
1:30.

²⁰By his divine revelation he broke open
    the hidden fountains of the deep,
    bringing secret springs to the surface
    as the mist of the night dripped down from heaven.ᵃ

Wisdom, Our Hiding Place

²¹My child, never drift off course from these two goals
    for your life:
    to walk in wisdom and to discover your purpose.ᵇ
    Don't ever forget how they empower you.
²²For they strengthen you inside and out
    and inspire you to do what's right;ᶜ
    you will be energized and refreshed by the healing
        they bring.
²³They give you living hope to guide you,
    and not one of life's tests will cause you to stumble.
²⁴You will sleep like a baby, safe and sound—
    your rest will be sweet and secure.
²⁵You will not be subject to terror, for it will not terrify
    you.
    Nor will the disrespectful be able to push you aside,ᵈ
²⁶because God is your confidence in times of crisis,
    keeping your heart at rest in every situation.ᵉ

---

a 3:20 The dew is a metaphor for the Holy Spirit, who comes from the heavens and drenches us with God's presence. See Gen. 27:28; Deut. 32:2; Judg. 6:37–40; Ps. 133:3.

b 3:21 Like many Hebrew words, there are various possible translations. The word translated here as "purpose" can also mean "discretion," "counsel," "meditation," or "discernment."

c 3:22 Or "adorn your neck." The neck is a picture of our will and conscience.

d 3:25 As translated from the Septuagint.

e 3:26 Or "keeping your foot from being caught."

Wisdom in Relationships

²⁷Why would you withhold payment on your debt*
when you have the ability to pay? Just do it!*
²⁸When your friend comes to ask you for a favor,
why would you say, "Perhaps tomorrow,"
when you have the money right there in your
pocket?
Help him today!
²⁹Why would you hold a grudge* in your heart
toward your neighbor who lives right next door?
³⁰And why would you quarrel with those
who have done nothing wrong to you?
Is that a chip on your shoulder?*
³¹Don't act like those bullies or learn their ways.
³²Every violent thug is despised by the Lord,
but every tender lover finds friendship with God
and will hear his intimate secrets.*
³³The wicked walk under God's constant curse,
but the righteous walk under a stream of his
blessing,
for they seek to do what is right.
³⁴If you walk with the mockers you will learn to mock,
but God's grace and favor flow to the meek.*
³⁵Stubborn fools fill their lives with disgrace,
but glory and honor rest upon the wise.

a 3:27 The Septuagint is "Why would you withhold from the poor
[those who need it]?"
b 3:27 The Hebrew text here literally means "Do not withhold wealth
from its owners." See Rom. 13:7.
c 3:29 Or "plot evil."
d 3:30 See Rom. 12:18.
e 3:32 See Ps. 25:14.
f 3:34 See James 4:6 and 1 Peter 5:5.

A Father's Instruction

4 Listen to my correction, my sons,
for I speak to you as your father.[a]
Let discernment enter your heart
and you will grow wise with the understanding I
impart.
[2]My revelation-truth[b] is a gift to you,
so remain faithful to my instruction.
[3]For I, too, was once the delight of my father[c]
and cherished by my mother—their beloved[d] child.
[4]Then my father taught me, saying,
"Never forget my words.
If you do everything that I teach you, you will reign
in life."[e]
[5]So make wisdom your quest—
search for the revelation of life's meaning.
Don't let what I say go in one ear and out the other.
[6]Stick with wisdom and she will stick to you,
protecting you throughout your days.
She will rescue all those who passionately listen to
her voice.[f]
[7]Wisdom is the most valuable commodity—so buy it!
Revelation-knowledge is what you need—so invest
in it!

---

a 4:1 Read and study this entire chapter as though it were Jesus Christ
speaking to you. He is the Father of Eternity, and we are called his
sons. See Isa. 9:6–7 and Rev. 21:6–7.

b 4:2 Literally "Torah."

c 4:3 See Matt. 17:5 and John 3:35.

d 4:3 Or "unique." See Luke 1–2.

e 4:4 The lessons of wisdom are meant to be passed on from parents
to children.

f 4:6 It is not enough to acquire wisdom; we must love her and listen
wholeheartedly to her instruction.

⁸Wisdom will exalt you when you exalt her truth.*a*
  She will lead you to honor and favor
  when you live your life by her insights.
⁹You will be adorned with beauty and grace,*b*
  and wisdom's glory will wrap itself around you,*c*
  making you victorious in the race.

Two Pathways

¹⁰My son, if you will take the time to stop and listen to
  me
  and embrace what I say,
  you will live a long and happy life
  full of understanding in every way.
¹¹I have taken you by the hand in wisdom's ways,
  pointing you to the path of integrity.
¹²Your progress will have no limits when you come
  along with me,
  and you will never stumble as you walk along the
    way.
¹³So receive my correction*d* no matter how hard it is to
  swallow,
  for wisdom will snap you back into place—
  her words will be invigorating life to you.
¹⁴Do not detour into darkness or even set foot on that
  path.

---

a 4:8 The Septuagint says, "Build a fort for wisdom and she will lift
you high."
b 4:9 Literally "She will place a garland of grace on your head and a
crown of beauty upon you." A garland and a crown are metaphors
for what is awarded a victor in a race. See 1 Cor. 9:24–25.
c 4:9 Or "wisdom's laurel of glory shielding you."
d 4:13 Wisdom will correct us and adjust our hearts to discipline.
We must embrace the corrections of wisdom in order to mature
spiritually.

¹⁵Stay away from it; don't even go there!
¹⁶For troublemakers are restless if they are not
   involved in evil.
   They are not satisfied until they have brought some-
      one harm.
¹⁷They feed on darkness and drink
   until they're drunk on the wine of wickedness.*a*
¹⁸But the lovers of God walk on the highway of light,*b*
   and their way shines brighter and brighter
   until the perfect day.
¹⁹But the wicked walk in thick darkness,
   like those who travel in fog,
   and yet don't have a clue why they keep stumbling!

Healing Words
²⁰Listen carefully, my dear child, to everything that I
   teach you,
   and pay attention to all that I have to say.
²¹Fill your thoughts with my words
   until they penetrate deep into your spirit.*c*
²²Then, as you unwrap my words,*d*
   they will impart true life and radiant health
   into the very core of your being.
²³So above all, guard the affections of your heart,*e*
   for they affect all that you are.

---

a 4:17 Or "violence."
b 4:18 Or "the glow of sunlight."
c 4:21 See Col. 3:16.
d 4:22 Or "discover my words."
e 4:23 The Hebrew word *levav* is the most common word for "heart." It
   includes our thoughts, our wills, our discernment, and our affections.

Pay attention to the welfare of your innermost
being,
for from there flows the wellspring*a* of life.
²⁴Avoid dishonest speech and pretentious words.
Be free from using perverse words no matter
what!

Watch Where You're Going
²⁵Set your gaze on the path before you.
With fixed purpose, looking straight ahead,
ignore life's distractions.^b
²⁶Watch where you're going!
Stick to the path of truth,
and the road will be safe and smooth before you.
²⁷Don't allow yourself to be sidetracked for even a
moment
or take the detour that leads to darkness.

Avoid Promiscuity
5 Listen to me, my son,
for I know what I'm talking about.
Listen carefully to my advice
²so that wisdom and discernment will enter your
heart,
and then the words you speak will express what
you've learned.

---

a 4:23 Although most translations have "the issues of life," the Hebrew
word *yasa* is actually "seasons," especially springtime. Out of your
heart flow the seasons of life. It is our hearts, not our ages or circumstances, that shape the seasons of our lives. If our hearts are tender
to God, we can live in perpetual springtime.
b 4:25 Implied in the text. See Heb. 12:1–2.

³Remember this:

    The lips of a seductress*ᵃ* seem sweet like honey,
    and her smooth words are like music in your ears.

⁴But I promise you this:

    In the end all you'll be left with is a bitter
      conscience.*ᵇ*
    For the sting of your sin will pierce your soul like a
      sword.

⁵She will ruin your life, drag you down to death,

    and lead you straight to hell.*ᶜ*

⁶She has prevented many from considering the paths
of life.

    Yes, she will take you with her where you don't want
      to go,
    sliding down a slippery road
    and not even realizing where the two of you will end
      up!

⁷Listen to me, young men,

    and don't forget this one thing I'm telling you—
    run away from her as fast as you can!

⁸Don't even go near the door of her house

    unless you want to fall into her seduction.

---

a 5:3 Some Jewish expositors view this "seductress" as a metaphor for heresy. She seduces, deceives, and drags to hell. For the believer, the seductress can be a picture of the false anointing of the religious spirit that attempts to seduce us, weaken our message, and rob the anointing of God from our ministries. Of course, there is also a clear and dire warning for all to stay sexually pure or face the consequences.

b 5:4 Or "*conscience* bitter as wormwood." See Rev. 8:10–11.

c 5:5 Or "Sheol." This is the Aramaic and Hebrew word for the place of the dead. The Greeks called it Hades. Sheol is not eternal: it will be destroyed. See Hos. 13:14 and Rev. 20:14.

⁹In disgrace you will relinquish your honor to another,
and all your remaining years will be squandered—
given over to the cruel one.ᵃ
¹⁰Why would you let strangers take away your
strengthᵇ
while the labors of your house go to someone else?
¹¹For when you grow old you will groan in anguish
and shameᶜ
as sexually transmitted diseases consume your body.ᵈ
¹²And then finally you'll admit that you were wrong
and say,
"If only I had listened to wisdom's voice
and not stubbornly demanded my own way,
because my heart hated to be told what to do!
¹³Why didn't I take seriously the warning of my wise
counselors?
Why was I so stupid to think that I could get away
with it?
¹⁴Now I'm totally disgraced and my life is ruined!
I'm paying the price—
for the people of the congregation are now my
judges."ᵉ

Sex Reserved for Marriage

¹⁵My son, share your love with your wife alone.
Drink from her well of pleasure and from no other.

---

a 5:9 This would be the devil, who torments the conscience as the
result of this sin.
b 5:10 Or "wealth." This could also refer to spiritual strength and
wealth.
c 5:11 The Hebrew word translated here as "groan" is also used for
the roar of a lion or the ocean's roar.
d 5:11 Implied in the context of the topic of sexual promiscuity. The
Hebrew word here means "diseases."
e 5:14 See John 8:1–11.

¹⁶Why would you have sex with a stranger
   or with anyone other than her?
¹⁷Reserve this pleasure for you and her alone and do
   not share it with another.ᵃ
¹⁸Your sex life will be blessedᵇ
   as you take joy and pleasure in the wife of your youth.
¹⁹Let her breasts be your satisfaction,ᶜ
   and let her embraceᵈ intoxicate you at all times.
   Be continually delighted and ravished with her love!
²⁰My son, why would you be exhilarated by an
   adulteress—
   by embracing a womanᵉ who is not yours?
²¹For God sees everything you do and his eyes are
   wide open
   as he observes every single habit you have.
²²Beware that your sins don't overtake you
   and that the scars of your own conscience don't
   become the ropes that tie you up.
²³Those who choose wickedness die for lack of
   self-control,
   for their foolish ways lead them astray,
   carrying them away as hostages—
   kidnapped captives robbed of destiny.

---

a 5:17 Because of the sudden change in the Hebrew text to the mas-
   culine gender ("stranger" or "another"), there is an inference that
   men having sex with men is forbidden, as well as sex with a woman
   who is not your wife.
b 5:18 The Hebrew phrase used here includes the word *fountain*,
   which is an obvious metaphor for the sex act. The root word for *fountain* can also refer to the eyes. It may be a poetic subtlety that your
   eyes should only be on your wife, not on the nakedness of another.
   See v. 19.
c 5:19 The Hebrew includes a picturesque metaphor of the wife being
   like a "friendly deer and a favored filly."
d 5:19 The Septuagint reads "let her share conversation with you."
e 5:20 Or "breasts."

Words of Wisdom

6 My son, if you cosign a loan for an acquaintance
and guarantee his debt,
  you'll be sorry that you ever did it!
²You'll be trapped by your promise
  and legally bound by the agreement.
  So listen carefully to my advice:
³Quickly get out of it if you possibly can!
  Swallow your pride, get over your embarrassment,
  and go tell your "friend" you want your name[a] off
    that contract.
⁴Don't put it off, and don't rest until you get it done.
⁵Rescue yourself from future pain[b]
  and be free from it once and for all.
  You'll be so relieved that you did![c]

Life Lessons

⁶When you're feeling lazy,
  come and learn a lesson from this tale of the tiny
    ant.
  Yes, all you lazybones, come learn
  from the example of the ant and enter into wisdom.
⁷The ants have no chief, no boss, no manager—
  no one has to tell them what to do.
⁸You'll see them working and toiling all summer long,
  stockpiling their food in preparation for winter.
⁹So wake up, sleepyhead. How long will you lie there?
  When will you wake up and get out of bed?

---

a 6:3 There is an implication in the Hebrew that the one whose loan
  was cosigned for is no longer a friend. The Hebrew word can also be
  translated "apostate."
b 6:5 The Hebrew word means "trap."
c 6:5 The life lesson to learn is that even when considering something
  that seems to be good, there may be unexpected consequences that
  should be considered before obligating yourself.

[10]If you keep nodding off and thinking, "I'll do it later,"
  or say to yourself, "I'll just sit back awhile and take
    it easy,"
  just watch how the future unfolds!
[11]By making excuses you'll learn what it means to go
  without.
  Poverty will pounce on you like a bandit[a]
  and move in as your roommate for life.[b]
[12-13]Here's another life lesson to learn
  from observing wayward and wicked men.[c]
  You can tell they are lawless.
  They're constant liars, proud deceivers,
  full of clever ploys and convincing plots.[d]
[14]Their twisted thoughts are perverse,
  and they are always scheming to stir up trouble,
  and sowing strife with every step they take.
[15]But when calamity comes knocking on their door,
  suddenly and without warning they're undone—
  broken to bits, shattered, with no hope of healing.[e]

---

a 6:11 Or "vagabond." The Hebrew phrase here is literally translated
   "one who walks (away)."
b 6:11 The life lesson from Solomon's parable is this: the ant only
   lives six months yet stores more food than it will ever consume. We
   should learn the wisdom of preparing for the future and frugality in
   the present. Don't put off for the future the preparations you should
   make today. Now is always better than later. Today is the day to
   choose what's right and serve the Lord.
c 6:12–13 The Hebrew word translated "wayward and wicked man"
   is actually "a man of Belial." This is a metaphor for a worthless man
   who worships other gods. The name Belial is found in numerous
   Dead Sea scrolls as a term for Satan.
d 6:12–13 The Hebrew gives a picture of those who "wink their eyes,
   shuffle their feet, and point their fingers." This is a figure of speech
   for the devious ways of the wicked.
e 6:15 The life lesson here is this: the clever and devious may look like
   they're getting ahead in life, but their path guarantees destruction,
   with no one to help them out of it.

Seven Things God Hates

¹⁶There are six evils God truly hates
and a seventh^a that is an abomination to him:
¹⁷Putting others down while considering yourself
superior,
spreading lies and rumors,
spilling the blood of the innocent,
¹⁸plotting evil in your heart toward another,
gloating over doing what's plainly wrong,
¹⁹spouting lies in false testimony,
and stirring up strife *between friends.*^b
These are entirely despicable to God!
²⁰My son, obey your father's godly instruction
and follow your mother's life-giving teaching.^c
²¹Fill your heart with their advice
and let your life be shaped by what they've taught
you.^d
²²Their wisdom will guide you wherever you go
and keep you from bringing harm to yourself.
Their instruction will whisper to you at every sunrise
and direct you through a brand-new day.
²³For truth^e is a bright beam of light
shining into every area of your life,
instructing and correcting you to discover the ways
to godly living.

---

a 6:16 The number seven is the number of fullness and completion. The poetic form here is stating that evil in its fullness is an abomination to God. The seven things are a description of the sin of man that stands in the temple of our bodies attempting to usurp God.

b 6:19 The Aramaic is "deception among brothers."

c 6:20 For the New Testament believer, our mother is the church, who nurtures us and feeds us life-giving words. See Gal. 4:21–31.

d 6:21 Or "Bind their words on your heart and tie them around your neck."

e 6:23 Or "Torah."

Truth or Consequences

24-25Truth will protect you from immorality
and from the promiscuity of another man's wife.
Your heart won't be enticed by her flatteries[a]
or lust over her beauty—
nor will her suggestive ways conquer you.
26Prostitutes reduce a man to poverty,[b]
and the adulteress steals your soul—
she may even cost you your life![c]
27For how can a man light his pants on fire and not be
burned?
28Can he walk over hot coals of fire[d] and not blister his
feet?
29What makes you think that you can sleep with
another man's wife
and not get caught?
Do you really think you'll get away with it?
Don't you know it will ruin your life?
30You can almost excuse a thief if he steals to feed his
own family.
31But if he's caught, he still has to pay back what he
stole sevenfold;
his punishment and fine will cost him greatly.
32Don't be so stupid as to think
you can get away with your adultery.
It will destroy your life,[e] and you'll pay the price
for the rest of your days.

---

a 6:24–25 Or "Don't let her captivate you with her fluttering eyelids."
b 6:26 Or "to beg for a loaf of bread."
c 6:26 The Hebrew phrase here is literally translated "she hunts for
your precious soul."
d 6:28 A picture of the lusts of the flesh.
e 6:32 Or "The destroyer of your soul will do this."

³³You'll discover what humiliation, shame,
and disgrace are all about,
for no one will ever let you forget what you've done.
³⁴A husband's jealousy makes a man furious;
he won't spare you when he comes to take revenge.
³⁵Try all you want to talk your way out of it—
offer him a bribe and see if you can manipulate him
with your money.
Nothing will turn him aside
when he comes to you with vengeance in his eyes!

Wisdom, Your True Love

7 Stick close to my instruction, my son,
and follow all my advice.
²If you do what I say you will live well.
Guard your life with my revelation-truth,
for my teaching is as precious as your eyesight.*ᵃ*
³Treasure my instructions, and cherish them within
your heart.*ᵇ*
⁴Say to wisdom, "I love you,"
and to understanding, "You're my sweetheart."
⁵"May the two of you protect me, and may we never
be apart!"
For they will keep you from the adulteress,
with her smooth words meant to seduce your heart.
⁶Looking out the window of my house one day
⁷I noticed among the mindless crowd
a simple, naïve young man who was about to go
astray.
⁸There he was, walking down the street.
Then he turned the corner,

---

a 7:2 Or "like you would the pupil of your eye." Literally "the little
man of the eye," which is a figure of speech for your most prized
possession.

b 7:3 Or "Write them upon the tablets of your heart."

going on his way hurrying to the house of the harlot—
the woman he had planned to meet.

[9]There he was in the twilight as darkness fell,
convinced no one was watching
as he entered the black shadows of hell.[a]

[10]That's when their rendezvous began.
A woman of the night appeared,
dressed to kill the strength of any man.
She was decked out as a harlot, pursuing her amorous plan.

[11]Her voice was seductive, rebellious, and boisterous
as she wandered far from what's right.

[12]Her type can be found soliciting on street corners
on just about any night.

[13]She wrapped her arms around the senseless young man
and held him tight—
she enticed him with kisses that seemed so right.
Then, with insolence, she whispered in his ear,

[14]"Come with me. It'll be all right.
I've got everything we need for a feast.
I'll cook you a wonderful dinner.[b]
So here I am—I'm all yours!

[15]You're the very one I've looked for,
the one I knew I wanted from the moment I saw you.
That's why I've come out here tonight,
so I could meet a man just like you.[c]

---

a 7:9 Implied from v. 27.

b 7:14 Or "offered peace offerings and paid my vows [in the temple]."
This is a way of saying, "I have lots of meat left over from the sacrifices I've offered, enough for a great meal."

c 7:15 Compared to Song. 3:1–4, this seems to be a parodic reversal
of the Shulamite who goes out into the city to seek a man, and when
she finds him, embraces him. This account of the harlot seems to be
the converse of the theme of Song of Songs.

¹⁶I've spread my canopy bed with coverings,
   lovely multicolored Egyptian linens
   ready for you to lie down on.
¹⁷I've sprinkled the sheets with intoxicating perfume
   made from myrrh, aloes, and sweet cinnamon.ᵃ
¹⁸Come, let's get comfortable and take pleasure in each
   other
   and make love all night!
¹⁹There's no one home, for my husband's away on
   business.
²⁰He left home loaded with money to spend,
   so don't worry.
   He won't be back until another month ends."ᵇ
²¹⁻²²He was swayed by her sophistication,
   enticed by her longing embrace.
   She led him down the wayward path right into sin
     and disgrace.
   Quickly he went astray, with no clue
   where he was truly headed,
   taken like a dumb ox alongside the butcher.
   She was like a venomous snake coiled to strike,
   so she set her fangs into him!ᶜ
²³He's like a man about to be executed with an arrow
   right through his heart—

ᵃ 7:17 Although these spices are found in the sacred anointing oil, the adulteress (religious system) has only a false anointing with no true power.

ᵇ 7:20 Or "He left with a bag of money and won't be back until the new moon."

ᶜ 7:21–22 The last sentence in this verse is arguably difficult to translate, with many variant options. The Aramaic is "taken like a dog to captivity." The Hebrew can be translated "bounding like a stag to a trap." Other ancient Jewish commentaries refer to this portion as "rushing like a venomous snake to discipline the foolish one," meaning that with the swiftness of a snake striking its prey, a fool lunges into his own destruction.

like a bird that flies into the net,
unaware of what's about to happen.
²⁴So listen to me, you young men.
You'd better take my words seriously!
²⁵Control your sexual urges and guard your hearts
against lust.
Don't let your passions get out of hand
and don't lock your eyes onto a beautiful woman.
Why would you want to even get close
to temptation and seduction,
to have an affair with her?
²⁶She has pierced the souls of multitudes of men—
many mighty ones have fallen
and have been brought down by her.ᵃ
²⁷If you're looking for the road to hell,
just go looking for her house!ᵇ

---

a 7:26 The Aramaic is even more descriptive: "She has slain a multitude of mighty ones; they've all been killed by her."

b 7:27 This parable (vv. 6–27) not only warns against the obvious evils of adultery and immorality, but also serves as a warning to the anointed young men in ministry not to be seduced by the religious system. Wisdom looks from the window (revelation and insight—see Ezek. 8) of her house (the true church of Jesus) and sees a young man (not fully mature—see 1 John 2:12–14) who has placed himself in the path of sin. This made him vulnerable to the seduction of the "harlot" system of a works-based religion that enticed him into her bed (partnership, covering, and ordination with her and her system—see Rev. 17–18) covered with Egyptian linens (Egypt is a picture of the world system that holds people in bondage). She is loud and stubborn (the old self-life never dealt with) and will not remain in her house (the true church of Jesus). She lives in the darkness of compromise and her ways are the ways of death. She doesn't remain faithful to her husband (the Bridegroom-God). The two women of Proverbs are the harlot mentioned here and the virtuous woman found in chapter 31, who speak of two systems of worship. One is true and virtuous; the other is false and seductive.

Wisdom Calling

8 ¹⁻³Can't you hear the voice of Wisdom?[a]
From the top of the mountains of influence
she speaks into the gateways of the glorious city.[b]
At the place where pathways merge,
at the entrance of every portal,
there she stands, ready to impart understanding,
shouting aloud to all who enter,
preaching her sermon to those who will listen.[c]
⁴"I'm calling to you, sons of Adam,
yes, and to you daughters as well.
⁵Listen to me and you will be prudent and wise.
For even the foolish and feeble can receive an
understanding heart
that will change their inner being.
⁶The meaning of my words will release within you
revelation
for you to reign in life.[d]
My lyrics will empower you to live by what is right.

---

a 8:1–3 Wisdom is personified throughout the book of Proverbs. Lady Wisdom is a figure of speech for God himself, who invites us to receive the best way to live, the excellent and noble way of life found in Jesus Christ. Jesus is wisdom personified, for he was anointed with the Spirit of Wisdom. See Isa. 11:1–2; 1 Cor. 1:30; Col. 2:3.

b 8:1–3 As translated from the Aramaic. The church is also a gateway, the house of God, the portal to heaven, and as Jesus calls it, a "city that stands on a hilltop" (see Matt. 5:14). Christ is the head of the church, where the wisdom of God is revealed. See 1 Cor. 1 and Eph. 3:10–12.

c 8:1–3 In chapter 7 it was the harlot calling out to the simple; here it is Lady Wisdom. True wisdom is easy to find—we only have to listen to her voice. Though it comes from above, it is found on street level. Creation and conscience are two voices that speak to our hearts. To discover wisdom, we don't need a brilliant intellect but a tender, attentive heart.

d 8:6 The Hebrew word is literally translated as "princely" or "noble" things. The implication is that these words of wisdom are for ruling and reigning in life.

⁷For everything I say is unquestionably true,
    and I refuse to endure the lies of lawlessness—
    my words will never lead you astray.
⁸All the declarations of my mouth can be trusted;
    they contain no twisted logic or perversion of the
       truth.
⁹All my words are clear and straightforward to everyone
    who possesses spiritual understanding.
    If you have an open mind, you will receive
      revelation-knowledge.
¹⁰My wise correction is more valuable than silver or
    gold.
    The finest gold is nothing compared to the
      revelation-knowledge
    I can impart."
¹¹Wisdom is so priceless that it exceeds the value of
    any jewel.ᵃ
    Nothing you could wish for can equal her.
¹²"For I am Wisdom, and I am shrewd and intelligent.
    I have at my disposal living-understanding
    to devise a plan for your life.ᵇ
¹³Wisdom pours into you
    when you begin to hate every form of evil in your life,
    for that's what worship and fearing God is all about.
    Then you will discover
    that your pompous pride and perverse speech
    are the very ways of wickedness that I hate!"

The Power of Wisdom
¹⁴"You will find true success when you find me,
    for I have insight into wise plans that are designed
      just for you.

---

a 8:11 Literally "corals" or "pearls."
b 8:12 Or "to discover clever inventions."

I hold in my hands living-understanding,[a] courage,
and strength.
[15]I empower kings to reign and rulers to make laws
that are just.[b]
[16]I empower princes to rise and take dominion,
and generous ones to govern the earth.[c]
[17]I will show my love to those who passionately love
me.[d]
For they will search and search continually until
they find me.
[18]Unending wealth and glory
come to those who discover where I dwell.
The riches of righteousness and a long, satisfying
life
will be given to them.[e]
[19]What I impart has greater worth than gold and
treasure,
and the increase I bring benefits more than a wind-
fall of income.
[20]I lead you into the ways of righteousness
to discover the paths of true justice.
[21]Those who love me gain great wealth[f] and a glorious
inheritance,
and I will fill their lives with treasures."

---

a 8:14 Or "I am living-understanding."

b 8:15 We have been made kings and priestly rulers by the grace of
redemption.

c 8:16 As translated from many Hebrew manuscripts and the Septuagint. Other Hebrew manuscripts have "and all nobles who govern
justly." The word *nobles* can also be translated "generous ones."

d 8:17 Wisdom is not found by the halfhearted. One must love wisdom
to gain it. A superficial desire will yield only a superficial knowledge.

e 8:18 Or "riches and righteousness." The phrase "a long, satisfying
life" is from the Aramaic.

f 8:21 The Aramaic is "I will leave great hope as an inheritance to my
friends."

Wisdom in the Beginning

²²"In the beginning I was there,
for God possessed me[a] even before he created the
universe.
²³From eternity past I was set in place,
before the world began.
I was anointed[b] from the beginning.
²⁴Before the oceans depths were poured out,
and before there were any glorious fountains
overflowing with water,[c]
I was there, dancing![d]
²⁵Even before one mountain had been sculpted
or one hill raised up,
I was already there, dancing!
²⁶When he created the earth, the fields,
even the first atom of dust,
I was already there.
²⁷When he hung the tapestry of the heavens
and stretched out the horizon of the earth,

---

a 8:22 The Aramaic and the Septuagint read "The Lord created me at
the beginning." The Hebrew verb translated here as "possessed" has
two basic meanings. One is "acquired," the other is "created." Poet-
ically, it is a statement that the existence of Wisdom (Christ) was not
independent of God at creation but was manifested and possessed
by God as he created all things. Otherwise, it would sound like God
was without wisdom before he created it.

b 8:23 The Hebrew word translated "anointed" here literally means
"poured out" and is often used to describe the anointing oil poured
out over a king.

c 8:24 The Hebrew uses the word *kabad*, which means "glory," to
describe the fountains. It could also be translated "fountains of
glory" or "glorious fountains."

d 8:24 Many translations have "I was born [or brought forth]." The
Hebrew word for "born" is taken from a word that means "to kick
and twirl" or "to dance."

²⁸when the clouds and skies were set in place
and the subterranean fountains began to flow strong,
I was already there.
²⁹When he set in place the pillars of the earth
and spoke the decrees of the seas,
commanding the waves
so that they wouldn't overstep their boundaries,
³⁰I was there, close to the Creator's side[a] as his master
artist.[b]
Daily he was filled with delight in me
as I playfully rejoiced before him.[c]
³¹I laughed and played,
so happy with what he had made,
while finding my delight in the children of men."[d]

Wisdom Worth Waiting For

³²"So listen, my sons and daughters, to everything I
tell you,
for nothing will bring you more joy than following
my ways.
³³Listen to my counsel,
for my instruction will enlighten you.
You'll be wise not to ignore it.
³⁴If you wait at wisdom's doorway,[e]
longing to hear a word for every day,
joy will break forth within you as you listen for what
I'll say.

---

a 8:30 See John 1:1.

b 8:30 Or "architect."

c 8:30 The Hebrew word translated here as "rejoiced" can also be
translated as "joyfully playing" or "laughing."

d 8:31 What a beautiful picture we find here of Wisdom (Christ), who
finds his fulfillment in us. See Pss. 8:4–9; 16:3; Eph. 2:10; 19–22;
Heb. 2:10.

e 8:34 Or "Guard the door of my entrances."

³⁵For the fountain of life pours into you every time that
you find me,
and this is the secret of growing in the delight
and the favor of the Lord.
³⁶But those who stumble and miss me will be sorry
they did!
For ignoring what I have to say will bring harm to
your own soul.
Those who hate me are simply flirting with death!"ᵃ

Wisdom's Feast

9 Wisdomᵇ has built herself a palaceᶜ
upon seven pillars to keep it secure.ᵈ
²She has made ready a banquet feast
and the sacrifice has been killed.ᵉ
She has mingled her wine, and the table's all set.ᶠ

---

a 8:36 To hate wisdom is not only a sign of stupidity, but it is also a
mark of depravity.

b 9:1 Lady Wisdom is a poetic personification representing Christ, the
Wisdom of God (1 Cor. 1:30). This is a classic form of a synecdo-
che. The Hebrew word *chokmah* ("wisdom") can also mean "sacred
sense." It is the understanding and insight given only by God.

c 9:1 There is a fascinating word play in the Hebrew text. The verb
meaning "to build" and the word translated "son" come from the
same root. "Build" is *banah* and "son" is *ben*. The house Wisdom is
building is a son. You and I are sons of God who are being built into
a spiritual house. There is also a verb in the Hebrew for "hewn" (as
in stones). We are living stones raised up to be God's temple. See Ps.
127:1; Matt. 7:24–27; 16:18; Heb. 3:5–6.

d 9:1 The seven pillars of wisdom (plural, "wisdoms") point us to the
seven days of creation, the seven spirits of God, and the seven com-
ponents of heavenly wisdom given in James 3:17–18.

e 9:2 As translated from the Aramaic. The sacrifice points us to Cal-
vary. Wisdom's pillar is a cross. The Hebrew phrase here literally
means "she has prepared her meat."

f 9:2 Wisdom's feast will teach us the ways of God. We feed our hearts
on revelation-truth that transforms us; then we implement with wise
strategies the understanding we have learned at the feasting table.

³She has sent out her maidens,
  crying out from the high place,
  inviting everyone to come
  and eat until they're full.
⁴"Whoever wants to know me and receive my wisdom,
⁵come and dine at my table and drink of my wine.
⁶Lay aside your simple thoughts and leave your paths
  behind.
  Agree with my ways, live in my truth,
  and you will find righteousness."
⁷If you try to correct an arrogant cynic,
  expect an angry insult in return.
  And if you try to confront an evil man,
  don't be surprised if all you get is a slap in the face!
⁸So don't even bother to correct a mocker,
  for he'll only hate you for it.
  But go ahead and correct the wise;
  they'll love you even more.ᵃ
⁹Teach a wise man what is right
  and he'll grow even wiser.
  Instruct the lovers of God
  and they'll learn even more.
¹⁰The starting point for acquiring wisdom
  is to be consumed with awe as you worship Yahweh.
  To receive the revelation of the Holy One,ᵇ
  you must come to the one who has
    living-understanding.
¹¹Wisdom will extend your life,
  making every year more fruitful than the one before.

---

a 9:8 See Ps. 141:5.
b 9:10 Literally "holy ones."

¹²So it is to your advantage to be wise.
But to ignore the counsel of wisdom
is to invite trouble into your life.*

A Spirit Named Foolish

¹³There is a spirit named Foolish,
who is boisterous and brash;
she's seductive and restless.
¹⁴And there she sits at the gateway to the high places,
on her throne overlooking the city.
¹⁵She preaches to all who walk by her
who are clueless as to what is happening:*
¹⁶"Come home with me."
She invites those who are easily led astray, saying,
¹⁷"Illicit sex is the best sex of all.
Our secret affair will be sweeter than all others."*
¹⁸Little do they know when they answer her call
that she dwells among the spirits of the dead,
and all her guests soon become citizens of hell!*

---

a 9:12 The Aramaic adds here "The liar feeds on the wind and chases fantasies, for he has forsaken what is true to travel in a barren wilderness; forgetting the right paths, he leaves his own vineyard to walk with thirst and gather nothing." The Septuagint adds here "If you forsake folly you will reign forever. Seek discretion and your understanding will bring you knowledge."

b 9:15 Or "who are walking straight ahead on their paths."

c 9:17 The Hebrew phrase here literally means "Stolen waters are sweet, and bread eaten in secret is pleasant." This is an obvious metaphor of finding sexual pleasure with someone other than your spouse and trying to get away with it. Finding pleasure in your relationship with your spouse is like drinking from a pure, clean fountain. But stolen water from someone else's fountain is yielding to foolishness. Adultery is always sin.

d 9:18 Older Aramaic and Septuagint manuscripts add a verse here not found in the Hebrew: "But turn away; linger not in the place or even look at her. Don't drink from a strange fountain. Abstain and drink not from an alien fountain, so that you will enjoy a long life."

Wisdom for Today

10 The wisdom of Solomon:[a]
When wisdom comes to a son,
joy comes to a father.
When a son turns from wisdom,
a mother grieves.
[2] Gaining wealth through dishonesty[b] is no gain at all.
But honesty brings you a lasting happiness.[c]
[3] The Lord satisfies the longings of all his lovers,[d]
but he withholds from the wicked what their souls
crave.[e]
[4] Slackers will know what it means to be poor,
while the hard worker becomes wealthy.
[5] Know the importance of the season you're in
and a wise son you will be.
But what a waste when an incompetent son
sleeps through his day of opportunity![f]
[6] The lover of God is enriched beyond belief,
but the evil man only curses his luck.[g]
[7] The reputation of the righteous
becomes a sweet memorial to him,
while the wicked life only leaves a rotten stench.[h]

---

a 10:1 The title of this section starting with Prov. 10 indicates a different form. Solomon's four hundred sayings of wisdom fill this section, going through 22:16. This compilation is an assorted collection of proverbs that is not easily outlined but is profound in its scope.

b 10:2 Or "the treasures of wickedness."

c 10:2 Or "Righteousness [honesty] delivers you from death."

d 10:3 Or "satisfies the souls of the righteous."

e 10:3 The Aramaic is "the property of the evil he demolishes."

f 10:5 Or "To gather in the summer is to be a wise son, but to sleep through the harvest is a disgrace."

g 10:6 The Hebrew is ambiguous and is literally translated "the mouth of the wicked covers violence."

h 10:7 Some Hebrew manuscripts and the Aramaic read "the name of the wicked will be extinguished."

⁸The heart of the wise will easily accept instruction.
But those who do all the talking
are too busy to listen and learn.
They'll just keep stumbling ahead
into the mess they created.
⁹The one who walks in integrity[a]
will experience a fearless confidence in life,
but the one who is devious
will eventually be exposed.
¹⁰The troublemaker always has a clever plan
and won't look you in the eye,
but the one who speaks correction honestly
can be trusted to make peace.[b]
¹¹The teachings of the lovers of God are like
living truth flowing from the fountain of life,
but the words of the wicked
hide an ulterior motive.[c]
¹²Hatred keeps old quarrels alive,[d]
but love draws a veil over every insult[e]
and finds a way to make sin disappear.
¹³Words of wisdom flow from the one with true
discernment.
But to the heartless, words of wisdom
become like rods beating their backside.
¹⁴Wise men don't divulge all that they know,[f]
but chattering fools blurt out words
that bring them to the brink of ruin.

---

a 10:9 Or "innocence." The Aramaic is "He who walks in perfection walks in hope."
b 10:10 As translated from the Septuagint. The Hebrew is "the babbling fool comes to ruin."
c 10:11 Or "hide violence."
d 10:12 The Aramaic is "Hatred stirs up judgment."
e 10:12 Love will cover up offenses against us, but never our own offenses.
f 10:14 Or "Those who are wise store up knowledge [like treasure]."

¹⁵A rich man's wealth becomes like a citadel of
strength,^{*a*}
  but the poverty of the poor leaves their security in
    shambles.
¹⁶The lovers of God earn their wages for a life of
righteousness,
  but the wages of the wicked are squandered on a
    life of sin.^{*b*}
¹⁷If you readily receive correction,
  you are walking on the path to life.
  But if you reject rebuke,
  you're guaranteed to go astray.^{*c*}
¹⁸The one who hides his hatred while pretending to be
your friend
  is nothing but a liar.
  But the one who slanders you behind your back
  proves that he's a fool, never to be trusted.
¹⁹If you keep talking, it won't be long
  before you're saying something really wrong.
  Prove you're wise from the very start—
  just bite your tongue and be strong!
²⁰The teachings of the godly ones are like pure silver,
  bringing words of redemption to others,^{*d*}
  but the heart of the wicked is corrupt.
²¹The lovers of God feed many with their teachings,^{*e*}
  but the foolish ones starve themselves
  for lack of an understanding heart.

---

a 10:15 Or "his fortified city."

b 10:16 Or "their harvest of wickedness."

c 10:17 The Aramaic is even more blunt: "Reject rebuke and you're a
moron!"

d 10:20 Or "The tongue of the just is like choice silver." Silver is a
metaphor for redemption.

e 10:21 The Aramaic is "The lips of the righteous multiply mercy."

²²True enrichment comes from the blessing of the Lord,
with rest and contentment*ᵃ* in knowing
that it all comes from him.
²³The fool*ᵇ* finds fun in planning to do wrong,
but the wise delight in having discernment.
²⁴The lawless are haunted by their fears
and what they dread will come upon them,*ᶜ*
but the longings of the lovers of God will all be
fulfilled.
²⁵The wicked are blown away by every stormy wind.
But when a catastrophe comes,
the lovers of God have a secure anchor.
²⁶To trust a lazy person to get a job done
will be as irritating as smoke in your eyes—
as enjoyable as a toothache!
²⁷Living in the worship and awe of God
will bring you many years of contented living.
So how could the wicked ever expect to have a long,
happy life?
²⁸Lovers of God have a joyful feast of gladness,
but the ungodly see their hopes vanish right before
their eyes.
²⁹The beautiful ways of God are a safe resting place
for those who have integrity.*ᵈ*
But to those who work wickedness
the ways of God spell doom.
³⁰God's lover can never be greatly shaken.
But the wicked will never inherit
the covenant blessings.*ᵉ*

---

a 10:22 Or "with no labor or sorrow attached."
b 10:23 The word translated "fool" means "moron" in the Aramaic.
c 10:24 This speaks of the consequences of sin. There is a Judge who
    sees all that we do and will call us to account one day.
d 10:29 The Aramaic is "The way of Yahweh is power to the perfect."
e 10:30 Or "land." This is metaphor for all of the covenantal blessings.

³¹The teachings of the righteous are loaded with
wisdom,
but the words of the evil ones are crooked and
perverse.
³²Words that bring delight pour from the lips of the
godly,
but the words of the wicked are duplicitous.

Living in Righteousness

11 Dishonest business practice*ᵃ*
is something that Yahweh truly hates.
But it pleases him when we apply the right standards
of measurement.*ᵇ*

stay
open +
curious

²When you act with presumption,
convinced that you're right,
don't be surprised if you fall flat on your face!
But humility leads to wisdom.
³Integrity will lead you to success,
but treachery will destroy your dreams.
⁴When judgment day comes,   *money < morals*
all the wealth of the world won't help you one bit.
So be rich in righteousness,
for that's the only thing that can save you in death.
⁵Those with good character walk on a smooth path,
with no detour or deviation.
But the wicked keep falling because of their own
wickedness.
⁶Integrity will keep a good man from falling.
But the unbeliever is trapped,
held captive to his sinful desires.

---

a 11:1 The Hebrew phrase here literally means "scales of deception
[false balances]."
b 11:1 The Hebrew phrase here literally means "a perfect stone."
Stones were used as the legitimate weights of balance. Jesus is the
perfect stone. See Rev. 2:17.

[handwritten: You only have your lifetime to work on this]

7When an evil man dies, all hope is lost,
  for his misplaced confidence goes in the coffin,
  buried along with him.
8The righteous are snatched away from trouble,
  and the wicked show up in their place.*a*
9The teachings of hypocrites can destroy you,
  but revelation-knowledge will rescue the righteous.*b*
10The blessing that rests on the righteous
  releases strength and favor to the entire city,*c*
  but shouts of joy will be heard when the wicked one
    dies.
11The blessing of favor resting upon the righteous
  influences a city to lift it higher,*d*
  but wicked leaders tear it apart by their words.
12To quarrel with a neighbor is senseless.*e*
  Bite your tongue; be wise and keep quiet!
13You can't trust gossipers with a secret;
  they'll just go blab it all.
  Put your confidence instead in a trusted friend,
  for he will be faithful to keep it in confidence.
14People lose their way without wise leadership,
  but a nation succeeds and stands in victory
  when it has many good counselors to guide it.
15The evil man will do harm when confronted by a
  righteous man,
  because he hates those who await good news.*f*

---

a 11:8 Haman is a classic example of this principle. See Est. 7:10;
  9:24–25.
b 11:9 Or "the righteous will be strengthened."
c 11:10 As translated from the Aramaic and the Septuagint.
d 11:11 Jesus describes the church as a city. See Matt. 5:14.
e 11:12 Or "To disparage your neighbor is being heartless."
f 11:15 As translated from the Aramaic and the Septuagint. The
  Hebrew is "You'll be ruined if you cosign for a stranger, and a hater
  of handshakes will be safe."

¹⁶A gracious, generous woman
  will be honored with a splendid[a] reputation,
  but the woman who hates the truth
  lives with disgrace[b] and is surrounded by men
  who are cutthroats, only greedy for money.[c]

deceptive behavior

¹⁷A man of kindness attracts favor,
  while a cruel man attracts nothing but trouble.[d]
¹⁸Evil people may get a short-term gain,[e]
  but to sow seeds of righteousness
  will bring a true and lasting reward.
¹⁹A son of righteousness[f] experiences the abundant
  life,
    but the one who pursues evil hurries to his own
      death.
²⁰The Lord can't stand the stubborn heart bent toward
  evil,
    but he treasures those whose ways are pure.[g]
²¹Assault your neighbor and you will certainly be
  punished,[h]
    but God will rescue the children of the godly.
²²A beautiful woman who abandons good morals
  is like a fine gold ring dangling from a pig's snout.

---

a 11:16 Or "glorious."
b 11:16 As translated from the older Aramaic and Septuagint texts, but
   not included in newer Hebrew manuscripts. There is an additional
   line added by the Aramaic and the Septuagint: "The lazy will lack,
   but the diligent support themselves financially."
c 11:16 The Septuagint is "the diligent obtain wealth."
d 11:17 The Hebrew text indicates this trouble could be physical,
   related to one's health.
e 11:18 Or "wages of deception."
f 11:19 As translated from one Hebrew manuscript, the Aramaic, and
   the Septuagint. Most Hebrew manuscripts have "The one who pursues righteousness."
g 11:20 Or "wholehearted."
h 11:21 As translated from the Aramaic and the Targum (Hebrew-
   Aramaic commentary).

²³True lovers of God are filled with longings
  for what is pleasing and good,
  but the wicked can only expect doom.
²⁴Generosity brings prosperity,
  but withholding from charity brings poverty.
²⁵Those who live to bless others
  will have blessings heaped upon them,
  and the one who pours out his life to pour out
    blessings
  will be saturated with favor.*ᵃ*
²⁶People will curse the businessman with no ethics,
  but the one with a social conscience receives praise
    from all.*ᵇ*

If you have a good thing share it

²⁷Living your life seeking what is good for others
  brings untold favor,
  but those who wish evil for others will find it coming
    back on them.
²⁸Keep trusting in your riches and down you'll go!
  But the lovers of God rise up like flowers in the
    spring.
²⁹The fool who brings trouble to his own family
  will be cut out of the will,
  and the family servant will do better than he.
³⁰But a life lived loving God bears lasting fruit,
  for the one who is truly wise wins souls.*ᶜ*
³¹If the righteous are barely saved,
  what's in store for all the wicked?*ᵈ*

---

a 11:25 The Hebrew phrase here literally means "The soul of blessing
will grow fat."
b 11:26 The Hebrew phrase here literally means "The one who withholds produce will be cursed, but blessing will be on the head of the
one who sells it."
c 11:30 As translated from the Hebrew. The Aramaic and the Septuagint read "the souls of violent ones will be removed."
d 11:31 As translated from the Septuagint. See 1 Peter 4:18.

It's Right to Live for God

12 To learn the truth you must long to be teachable,[a]
or you can despise correction and remain
ignorant.

[2] If your heart is right, favor flows from the Lord,
but a devious heart invites his condemnation.

[3] You can't expect success by doing what's wrong.
But the lives of his lovers are deeply rooted and
firmly planted.

[4] The integrity and strength of a virtuous wife[b]
transforms her husband into an honored king.[c]
But the wife who disgraces her husband
weakens the strength of his identity.[d]

[5] The lovers of God are filled with good ideas
that are noble and pure,
but the schemes of the sinner
are crammed with nothing but lies.

[6] The wicked use their words to ambush and accuse,[e]
but the lovers of God speak to defend and protect.

[7] The wicked are taken out, gone for good,
but the godly families shall live on.

[8] Everyone admires a man of principles,
but the one with a corrupt heart is despised.

← Take responsibility

---

a 12:1 There are times when even the wise need correction, but they
will appreciate its value.

b 12:4 There is an amazing Hebrew word used here. It is more commonly
used to describe warriors, champions, and mighty ones. Many translations read "an excellent wife." But the meaning of the Hebrew word
chayil is better translated "an army that is wealthy," "strong," "mighty,"
"powerful," "with substance," "valiant," "virtuous," or "worthy."

c 12:4 Or "An excellent wife is the crown of her husband." By implication, her dignity makes him a king.

d 12:4 Or "she is like cancer in his bones." Bones are a metaphor for
inner strength, our inner being, or identity.

e 12:6 Or "lie in wait for blood." This is a figure of speech for
accusation.

⁹Just be who you are and work hard for a living,
　　for that's better than pretending to be important
　　and starving to death.
¹⁰A good man takes care of the needs of his pets,
　　while even the kindest acts of a wicked man are still
　　　cruel.
¹¹Work hard at your job and you'll have what you need.
　　Following a get-rich-quick scheme is nothing but a
　　　fantasy.
¹²The cravings of the wicked are only for what is evil,ᵃ
　　but righteousness is the core motivation for the
　　　lovers of God,
　　and it keeps them content and flourishing.ᵇ

[handwritten margin note: Thieves crave the loot + life vehicles]

Wisdom Means Being Teachable
¹³The wicked will get trapped by their words
　　of gossip, slander, and lies.ᶜ
　　But for the righteous, honesty is its own defense.
¹⁴For there is great satisfaction in speaking the truth,
　　and hard work brings blessings back to you.
¹⁵A fool is in love with his own opinion,
　　but wisdom means being teachable.

Learning to Speak Wisely
¹⁶If you shrug off an insult and refuse to take offense,
　　you demonstrate discretion indeed.ᵈ
　　But the fool has a short fuse
　　and will immediately let you know when he's
　　　offended.

[handwritten margin note: Let things go!]

ᵃ 12:12 As translated from the Septuagint. The Hebrew is "Thieves crave the loot of other thieves."
ᵇ 12:12 The meaning of the Hebrew text of v. 12 is uncertain.
ᶜ 12:13 The Hebrew is simply "sinful words," which implies gossip, slander, and lies.
ᵈ 12:16 Or "A shrewd man conceals his shame."

¹⁷Truthfulness marks the righteous,
  but the habitual liar can never be trusted.
¹⁸Reckless words are like the thrusts of a sword,
  cutting remarks meant to stab and to hurt.
  But the words of the wise soothe and heal.
¹⁹Truthful words will stand the test of time,
  but one day every lie will be seen for what it is.
²⁰Deception fills the hearts of those who plot harm,
  but those who plan for peace^a are filled with joy.
²¹Calamity is not allowed to overwhelm the righteous,
  but there's nothing but trouble waiting for the wicked.
²²Live in the truth and keep your promises,
  and the Lord will keep delighting in you,
  but he detests a liar.
²³Those who possess wisdom don't feel the need
  to impress others with what they know,
  but foolish ones make sure their ignorance is on
    display.
²⁴If you want to reign in life,^b *(SENSI)* *Take right action*
  don't sit on your hands.
  Instead, work hard at doing what's right,
  for the slacker will end up working to make some-
    one else succeed.
²⁵Anxious fear brings depression, *Think of positive things*
  but a life-giving word of encouragement
  can do wonders to restore joy to the heart.^c
  focus on positive/what makes you happy

---

a 12:20 Or "counselors of peace."
b 12:24 The Hebrew word for "reign" (*mashal*) is the title of the book: Proverbs. See introduction and the footnote on Prov. 1:1.
c 12:25 This insightful proverb can also be translated "Stop worrying! Think instead of what brings you gladness." Our focus must never be on what we can't change but on the everlasting joy we have in Christ. Sometimes we have to find the life-giving word of encouragement rising up in our own hearts. This is the secret of finding perpetual encouragement by the Word that lives in us.

²⁶Lovers of God give good advice to their friends,[a]
   but the counsel of the wicked will lead them astray.
²⁷A passive person won't even complete a project,
   but a passionate person makes good use
   of his time, wealth, and energy.[b]
²⁸Abundant life is discovered by walking in
   righteousness,
   but holding on to your anger leads to death.[c]

Living Wisely

13 A wise son or daughter desires a father's
   discipline,
   but the know-it-all never listens to correction.
²The words of the wise are kind and easy to swallow,
   but the unbeliever just wants to pick a fight and
      argue.
³Guard your words and you'll guard your life,
   but if you don't control your tongue,
   it will ruin everything.

Focus your effort

⁴The slacker wants it all and ends up with nothing,
   but the hard worker ends up with all that he longed
      for.
⁵Lovers of God hate what is phony and false,
   but the wicked are full of shame and behave
      shamefully.[d]

avoid deceptive stuff, biz, people

---

a 12:26 As translated from older Aramaic manuscripts. The Hebrew is
   uncertain.
b 12:27 Implied in the text, paraphrased from an uncertain Hebrew
   phrase. An alternate translation would be "A lazy person won't get
   to roast the game he caught, but the wealth of a diligent person is
   precious."
c 12:28 As translated from the Septuagint and the Aramaic. The
   Hebrew is uncertain.
d 13:5 The Hebrew word used here literally means "to cause a stink"
   or "to emit an odor." This is a figure of speech for what is shameful.

⁶Righteousness is like a shield of protection,
  guarding those who keep their integrity,
  but sin is the downfall of the wicked.
⁷One pretends to be rich but is poor.
  Another pretends to be poor but is quite rich.ᵃ
⁸The self-assurance of the rich is their money,ᵇ
  but people don't kidnap and extort the poor!
⁹The virtues of God's lovers shine brightly in the
  darkness, *Spirituality keeps you strong*
  but the flickering lamp of the ungodly will be
  extinguished.

Living frugal is Protection

Don't make money just to buy nice things

wisdom > pride

¹⁰Wisdom opens your heart to receive wise counsel,
  but pride closes your ears to advice
  and gives birth only to quarrels and strife.
¹¹Wealth quickly gained is quickly wastedᶜ—
  easy come, easy go!
  But if you gradually gain wealth,
  you will watch it grow.

Avoid quick riches

¹²When hope's dream seems to drag on and on,
  the delay can be depressing.
  But when at last your dream comes true,
  life's sweetness will satisfy your soul.ᵈ

Act fast on your dreams & avoid spinning wheels

¹³Despise the word, will you?
  Then you'll pay the price and it won't be pretty!
  But the one who honors the Father's holy
    instructions
  will be rewarded.
¹⁴When the lovers of God teach you truth,
  a fountain of life opens up within you,

---

a 13:7 It is never godly to be a phony. It's always better to be who you
   are and avoid pretense.
b 13:8 The Aramaic is "The salvation of the soul is a man's true
   wealth."
c 13:11 Or "Wealth gained by fraud will dwindle."
d 13:12 Or "it is a tree of life."

and their wise instruction will deliver you from the
ways of death.
[15]Everyone admires a wise, sensible person,
but the treacherous walk on the path of ruin.[a]
[16]Everything a wise and shrewd man does
comes from a source of revelation-knowledge,[b]
but the behavior of a fool puts foolishness on
parade![c]
[17]An undependable messenger causes a lot of trouble,
but the trustworthy and wise messengers
release healing wherever they go.[d]
[18]Poverty and disgrace come to the one
who refuses to hear criticism.[e]
But the one who is easy to correct is on the path of
honor.
[19]When God fulfills your longings,
sweetness fills your soul.
But the wicked refuse to turn from darkness
to see their desires come to pass.[f]
[20]If you want to grow in wisdom,
spend time with the wise.
Walk with the wicked
and you'll eventually become just like them.
[21]Calamity chases the sin-chaser,
but prosperity pursues the God-lover.

---

a 13:15 As translated from the Aramaic and the Septuagint. The
Hebrew is uncertain.
b 13:16 Or "A wise person thinks ahead."
c 13:16 The implication is that the fool is unable to finish anything he
begins.
d 13:17 God's sons and daughters are peacemakers, healers, and
faithful deliverers for others.
e 13:18 As translated from the Hebrew. The Septuagint is "Instruction
removes poverty and disgrace."
f 13:19 Implied by the Hebrew parallelism of the text.

²²The benevolent man leaves an inheritance
   that endures to his children's children,
   but the wealth of the wicked is treasured up for the
      righteous.
²³The lovers of God will live a long life and get to
   enjoy their wealth,
   but the ungodly will suddenly perish.ᵃ
²⁴If you withhold correction and punishmentᵇ from
   your children,
   you demonstrate a lack of true love.
   So prove your love and be prompt to punish them.ᶜ
²⁵The lovers of God will have more than enough,
   but the wicked will always lack what they crave.

The House of Wisdom

14 Every wise woman encourages and builds up her
   family,
   but a foolish woman over time will tear it down by
      her own actions.
²Lovers of truth follow the right path
   because of their wonderment and worship of God.
   But the devious display their disdain for him.
³The words of a proud fool will all come back to haunt
   him.
   But the words of the wise
   will become a shield of protection around them.

---

a 13:23 As translated from the Septuagint. The Hebrew is "In the fal-
low ground of the poor there is abundance of food, but injustice
sweeps it away." The Aramaic is "Those who don't find the way of
life destroy many years of wealth, and some are utterly destroyed."
There is a vast difference in the three translations. This translation
follows the Septuagint.

b 13:24 Or "spare the rod." Corporal punishment was common in premodern societies.

c 13:24 Or "The one who spares the rod hates his child."

handwritten margin note: mistakes, chaos, problems, happen—accept this

⁴The only clean stable is an empty stable.
  So if you want the work of an ox and to enjoy an
    abundant harvest,
  you'll have a mess or two to clean up!
⁵An honest witness will never lie,
  but a deceitful witness lies with every breath.
⁶The intellectually arrogant seek for wisdom,
  but they never seem to discover
  what they claim they're looking for.
  For revelation-knowledge flows to the one
  who hungers for understanding.
⁷The words of the wise are like weapons of
  knowledge.*ᵃ*
  If you need wise counsel, stay away from the fool.
⁸For the wisdom of the wise will keep life on the right
    track,
  while the fool only deceives himself
  and refuses to face reality.
⁹Fools mock the need for repentance,*ᵇ*
  while the favor of God rests upon all his lovers.
¹⁰Don't expect anyone else to fully understand
  both the bitterness and the joys
  of all you experience in your life.
¹¹The household of the wicked is soon torn apart,
  while the family of the righteous flourishes.
¹²You can rationalize it all you want
  and justify the path of error you have chosen,
  but you'll find out in the end that you took the road
    to destruction.
¹³Superficial laughter can hide a heavy heart,
  but when the laughter ends, the pain resurfaces.

---

a 14:7 As translated from the Aramaic.
b 14:9 Or "Fools mock guilt [or guilt offering]." The Septuagint is "The
house of the transgressor owes purification."

¹⁴Those who turn from the truth get what they deserve,
   but a good person receives a sweet reward.^a
¹⁵A gullible person will believe anything,
   but a sensible person will confirm the facts.
¹⁶A wise person is careful in all things and turns
      quickly from evil,
   while the impetuous fool moves ahead with
      overconfidence.
¹⁷An impulsive person has a short fuse and can ruin
      everything,
   but the wise show self-control.^b
¹⁸The naïve demonstrate a lack of wisdom,
   but the lovers of wisdom are crowned with
      revelation-knowledge.
¹⁹Evil ones will pay tribute to good people
   and eventually come to be servants of the godly.^c
²⁰The poor are disliked even by their neighbors,
   but everyone wants to get close to the wealthy.
²¹It's a sin to despise one who is less fortunate than
      you,^d
   but when you are kind to the poor,
   you will prosper and be blessed.
²²Haven't you noticed how evil schemers always wander astray?

---

a 14:14 As translated from Hebrew manuscripts. The Aramaic is "a good man will be filled from the awe of his soul."

b 14:17 As translated from the Aramaic. The Hebrew is "and a crafty schemer is hated." The Greek Septuagint is "a sensible man bears up under many things."

c 14:19 The Hebrew phrase literally means "they will come [or bow] at the gates of the righteous."

d 14:21 Implied in the Hebrew parallelism. The Hebrew phrase here literally means "your neighbor."

But kindness and truth come to those
who make plans to be pure in all their ways.[a]
²³If you work hard at what you do,
great abundance will come to you.
But merely talking about getting rich
while living to only pursue your pleasures[b]
brings you face-to-face with poverty.[c]
²⁴The true net worth of the wise[d] is the wealth that
wisdom imparts.
But the way of life for the fool is his foolishness.[e]
²⁵Speak the truth and you'll save souls,
but in the spreading of lies treachery thrives.
²⁶Confidence and strength flood the hearts
of the lovers of God who live in awe of him,
and their devotion provides their children
with a place of shelter and security.[f]
²⁷To worship God in wonder and awe
opens a fountain of life within you,
empowering you to escape death's domain.[g]
²⁸A king glories in the number of his loyal followers,
but a dwindling population spells ruin for any
leader.

> consider business)

---

a 14:22 Both the Aramaic and the Septuagint insert a verse here that
is not found in the Hebrew: "The followers of evil don't understand
mercy and faith, but you'll find kindness and faith with those who
do good."

b 14:23 As translated from the Septuagint.

c 14:23 There is an additional verse found here in the Aramaic that is
missing from the Hebrew text: "The Lord Yahweh heals every sickness, but evil speaking makes you sick [harms you]."

d 14:24 Or "the crown of the wise."

e 14:24 The Aramaic word translated here as "foolishness" can also
mean "insanity."

f 14:26 To live as a passionate lover of God will bring benefit even to
your children.

g 14:27 Or "empowering you to turn from the deadly snares."

²⁹When your heart overflows with understanding
you'll be very slow to get angry.
But if you have a quick temper,
your impatience will be quickly seen by all.
³⁰A tender, tranquil heart will make you healthy,ᵃ
but jealousy can make you sick.
³¹Insult your Creator, will you?
That's exactly what you do
every time you oppress the powerless!ᵇ
Showing kindness to the poor is equal to honoring
your maker.
³²The wicked are crushed by every calamity,
but the righteous find a strong hope
in the time of death.ᶜ
³³Wisdom soothes the heart of the one with
living-understanding,
but the heart of the fool just stockpiles stupidity.
³⁴A nation is exalted by the righteousness of its people,
but sin heaps disgrace upon the land.
³⁵A wise and faithful servant receives promotion from
the king,
but the one who acts disgracefully
gets to taste the anger of the king.ᵈ

---

a 14:30 Or "A heart of healing is the life of the flesh."
b 14:31 Or "slander the poor." Every human being is made in God's
image, including the poor.
c 14:32 As translated from the Masoretic Text. Our strong hope is that
our lives will continue in the presence of God in the resurrection
glory. Both the Septuagint and the Aramaic read quite differently:
"but the righteous have a refuge in their integrity."
d 14:35 As translated from the Hebrew. The Septuagint reads "and by
his good behavior shame is removed."

Wisdom Far Better than Wickedness

15 Respond gently when you are confronted
and you'll defuse the rage of another.
Responding with sharp, cutting words*ᵃ* will only
make it worse.
Don't you know that being angry
can ruin the testimony of even the wisest of men?*ᵇ*

²When wisdom speaks, understanding becomes
attractive.
But the words of the fool make their ignorance look
laughable.*ᶜ*

³The eyes of the Lord*ᵈ* are everywhere
and he takes note of everything that happens.
He watches over his lovers,
and he also sees the wickedness of the wicked.

⁴When you speak healing words,
you offer others fruit from the tree of life.
But unhealthy, negative words do nothing but crush
their hopes.*ᵉ*

⁵You're stupid to mock the instruction of a father,
but welcoming correction will make you brilliant.*ᶠ*

⁶There is prosperity in the house of the righteous,*ᵍ*
but the house of the wicked is filled with trouble,
no matter how much money they have.

---

a 15:1 Or "painful words."
b 15:1 This sentence is found only in the Septuagint.
c 15:2 The Aramaic reads "The mouths of fools vomit a curse."
d 15:3 "The eyes of the Lord" can also be a metaphor for his prophets.
e 15:4 Or "perverse words are the crushing of the spirit."
f 15:5 The Septuagint adds a verse that is not found in the Hebrew:
"In great righteousness there is great strength. But the ungodly will
one day perish from the earth."
g 15:6 The Septuagint and the Aramaic read "There is power in the
house of the righteous." Both concepts are valid.

[7]When wisdom speaks, revelation-knowledge is
   released,[a]
   but finding true wisdom in the word of a fool is
   futile.
[8]It is despicable to the Lord
   when people use the worship of the Almighty
   as a cloak for their sin,[b]
   but every prayer of the righteous is pleasing to his
   heart.
[9]The Lord detests the lifestyle of the wicked,
   but he loves those who pursue purity.[c]
[10]Severe punishment awaits the one
   who turns away from the truth,
   and those who rebel against correction will die.
[11]Even hell itself holds no secrets from the Lord God,
   for before his eyes, all is exposed—
   and so much more the heart of every human being.
[12]The know-it-all never esteems the one who tries to
   correct him.
   He refuses to seek good advice from the wise.[d]

Living an Ascended Life

[13]A cheerful heart puts a smile on your face,
   but a broken heart leads to depression.
[14]Lovers of God[e] hunger after truth,
   but those without understanding
   feast on foolishness and don't even realize it.

---

a 15:7 Or "is scattered like seed."

b 15:8 Or "the sacrifice of the wicked"; that is, worshiping God with a
   wicked heart, only to hide sin. Our yielded hearts must be the sacrifice we offer to God.

c 15:9 The Aramaic reads "he shows mercy to the one who practices
   righteousness."

d 15:12 Another way to say this is "The one who hates authority has
   no love for being taught."

e 15:14 Or "The upright" (Aramaic).

¹⁵Everything seems to go wrong
  when you feel weak and depressed.
  But when you choose to be cheerful,
  every day will bring you more and more joy and
    fullness.ᵃ
¹⁶It's much better to live simply,
  surrounded in holy awe and worship of God,
  than to have great wealth with a home full of
    trouble.
¹⁷It's much better to have a meal of vegetables sur-
    rounded with love and grace
  than a steak where there is hate.
¹⁸A touchy, hot-tempered man picks a fight,
  but the calm, patient man knows how to silence
    strife.
¹⁹Nothing seems to work rightᵇ for the lazy man,
  but life seems smooth and easy when your heart is
    virtuous.
²⁰When a son learns wisdom,
  a father's heart is glad.
  But the man who shamesᶜ his mother is a foolish son.
²¹The senseless fool treats life like a joke,
  but the one with living-understanding makes good
    choices.
²²Your plans will fall apart right in front of you
  if you fail to get good advice.
  But if you first seek out multiple counselors,
  you'll watch your plans succeed.
²³Everyone enjoys giving great advice.
  But how delightful it is to say the right thing at the
    right time!

See cut
Multiple counselors
get good advice
for your plans

ᵃ 15:15 The Septuagint reads quite differently: "And the good [heart]
  is always calm."
ᵇ 15:19 Or "The way is blocked with thorns."
ᶜ 15:20 Or "despises."

Care & thought for Future

²⁴The life-paths of the prudent lift them progressively
heavenward,
 delivering them from the death spirals
 that keep tugging them downward.
²⁵The Lord champions the widow's cause,^{*a*}
 but watch him as he smashes down the houses of
 the haughty!
²⁶The Lord detests wicked ways of thinking,^{*b*}
 but he enjoys lovely and delightful words.
²⁷The one who puts earning money above his family
 will have trouble at home,
 but those who refuse to exploit others
 will live *in peace*.
²⁸Lovers of God think before they speak,
 but the careless blurt out wicked words meant to
 cause harm.
²⁹The Lord doesn't respond to the wicked,
 but he's moved to answer the prayers of the
 righteous.

Stay positive

³⁰Eyes that focus on what is beautiful bring joy to the
 heart,^{*c*} *look on the bright side*
 and hearing a good report
 refreshes and strengthens the inner being.^{*d*}
³¹Accepting constructive criticism
 opens your heart to the path of life,
 making you right at home among the wise.
³²Refusing constructive criticism shows
 you have no interest in improving your life,

---

a 15:25 Or "The Lord maintains the boundaries of the widow."
b 15:26 Or "the thoughts of the wicked."
c 15:30 As translated from the Septuagint. The Hebrew is "The light of
the eyes brings joy."
d 15:30 The Hebrew here literally means "makes fat your bones."
Bones picture our inner being.

for revelation-insight only comes as you accept
  correction
and the wisdom that it brings.
³³The source of revelation-knowledge is found
  as you fall down in surrender before the Lord.
Don't expect to see Shekinah glory
  until the Lord sees your sincere humility.^a

[handwritten margin note: Turn yself ou to guidance]

[handwritten margin note: Be humble - you dont know everything]

Wisdom Exalts God

16 Go ahead and make all the plans you want,
  but it's the Lord who will ultimately direct your
  steps.^b
²We are all in love with our own opinions,
  convinced they're correct.
  But the Lord is in the midst of us,^c
  testing and probing our every motive.
³Before you do anything,
  put your trust totally in God and not in yourself.^d
  Then every plan you make will succeed.
⁴The Lord works everything together to accomplish his
  purpose.^e
  Even the wicked are included in his plans—
  he sets them aside for the day of disaster.
⁵Yahweh detests all the proud^f of heart,
  for pride attracts his punishment—

---

a 15:33 Or "Before honor is humility." The Hebrew uses the word
  kabod, which is translated as "glory" 156 times in the Old Testament.

b 16:1 As translated from the Septuagint. The Hebrew and Aramaic
  read "the Lord gives the right reply."

c 16:2 Or "in the midst of spirits."

d 16:3 Or "commit your business to God."

e 16:4 Or "for its answer."

f 16:5 The Hebrew word for "proud" is *gavah*, which comes from a
  root word that means "locust" (as a reference to a locust swarm that
  devours all the crops). Pride is like a locust swarm that always hin-
  ders a true spiritual harvest within us.

and you can count on that!

⁶You can avoid evil through surrendered worship
and the fear of God,
   for the power of his faithful love
   removes sin's guilt and grip over you.
⁷When the Lord is pleased with the decisions you've
   made,
   he activates grace to turn enemies into friends.
⁸It is better to have little with a heart that loves justice
   than to be rich and not have God on your side.
⁹Within your heart you can make plans for your future,
   but the Lord chooses the steps you take to get there.

Living like a King

¹⁰A king speaks the revelation of truth,
   so he must be extraordinarily careful in the decrees
   that he makes.
¹¹The Lord expects you to be fair in every business
   deal,
   for he is the one who sets the standards for
   righteousness.ᵃ
¹²Kings and leaders despise wrongdoing,
   for the true authority to rule and reign
   is built on a foundation of righteousness.
¹³Kings and leaders love to hear godly counsel,
   and they love those who tell them the truth.
¹⁴The anger of a king releases the messenger of
   death,ᵇ
   but a wise person will know how to pacify his wrath.
¹⁵Life-giving light streams from the presence of a king,ᶜ

---

a 16:11 Or "Honesty with scales and balances is the way of the Lord,
for all the stones in the bag are established by him."
b 16:14 See 1 Kings 2:25, 29–34, 46.
c 16:15 The Septuagint reads "The king's son is in the light of life."

and his favor is showered upon those who please
   him.
[16]Everyone wants gold, but wisdom's worth[a] is far
   greater.
   Silver is sought after,
   but a heart of understanding yields a greater return.
[17]Repenting from evil places you on the highway of
   holiness.
   Protect purity and you protect your life.[b]
[18]Your boast becomes a prophecy of a future failure.
   The higher you lift yourself up in pride,[c]
   the harder you'll fall in disgrace.
[19]It's better to be meek and lowly and live among the
   poor
   than to live high and mighty among the rich and
      famous.
[20]One skilled in business discovers prosperity,
   but the one who trusts in God is blessed beyond belief!

Walking with Wisdom

[21]The one with a wise heart is called "discerning,"
   and speaking sweetly to others
   makes your teaching even more convincing.
[22]Wisdom is a deep well of understanding
   opened up within you as a fountain of life for others,
   but it's senseless to try to instruct a fool.
[23]Winsome words pour from a heart of wisdom,

---

a 16:16 The Septuagint is "nests of wisdom."

b 16:17 There are two proverbs inserted here in the Septuagint that
   are not found in the Hebrew or Aramaic: "Receive instruction and
   you'll be prosperous; he who listens to correction shall be made
   wise." "He who guards his ways preserves his own soul; he who
   loves his life will watch his words."

c 16:18 Or "overconfidence."

adding value to all you teach.
²⁴Nothing is more appealing
than speaking beautiful, life-giving words.
For they release sweetness to our souls
and inner healing to our spirits.ᵃ
²⁵Before every person there is a path
that seems like the right one to take,
but it leads straight to hell!ᵇ
²⁶Life motivation comes from the deep longings of the heart,
and the passion to see them fulfilled urges you onward.ᶜ
²⁷A wicked scoundrel wants to dig up dirt on others,
only to spread slander and shred their reputation.
²⁸A twisted person spreads rumors;
a whispering gossip ruins good friendships.
²⁹A vicious criminal can be persuasive,
enticing others to join him as partners in crime,
but he leads them all down a despicable path.
³⁰It's easy to tell when a wicked man
is hatching some crooked scheme—
it's written all over his face.
His looks betray him as he gives birth to his sin.
³¹Old age with wisdom will crown you with dignity and honor,ᵈ
for it takes a lifetime of righteousness to acquire it.
³²Do you want to be a mighty warrior?

---

a 16:24 Or "healing to the bones." Bones are a metaphor for our inner being.
b 16:25 As translated from the Septuagint. The Hebrew is "the ways of death."
c 16:26 The meaning of the Hebrew in this verse is uncertain.
d 16:31 Or "Gray hair is a crown of splendor." In the Hebrew culture the old were honored above all, especially if they acquired wisdom. See Lev. 19:32.

It's better to be known as one who is patient and
  slow to anger.*a*
Do you want to conquer a city?
Rule over your temper before you attempt to rule a
  city.
³³We may toss the coin and roll the dice,
  but God's will is greater than luck.*b*

Wisdom's Virtues

17 A simple, humble life with peace and quiet
  is far better than an opulent lifestyle with nothing
  but quarrels and strife at home.
²A wise, intelligent servant will be honored above a
  shameful son.
  He'll even end up having a portion left to him in his
    master's will.
³In the same way that gold and silver are refined by
  fire,
  the Lord purifies your heart by the tests and trials of
    life.
⁴Those eager to embrace evil listen to slander,
  for a liar loves to listen to lies.
⁵Mock the poor, will you?
  You insult your Creator every time you do!
  If you make fun of others' misfortune,
  you'd better watch out—your punishment is on its
    way.
⁶Grandparents have the crowning glory of life:

---

a 16:32 The Septuagint is "It's better to be forgiving than strong."
b 16:33 Or "Into the center the lot is cast and from Yahweh is all its
  judgment." The casting of lots was a common form of divination in
  premodern societies.

grandchildren!
And it's only proper for children to take pride in
their parents.[a]
[7]It is not proper for a leader to lie and deceive,
and don't expect excellent words to be spoken by a
fool.[b]
[8]Wise instruction[c] is like a costly gem.
It turns the impossible into success.
[9]Love overlooks the mistakes of others,
but dwelling on the failures of others devastates
friendships.
[10]One word of correction breaks open a teachable
heart,
but a fool can be corrected a hundred times
and still not know what hit him.
[11]Rebellion thrives in an evil man,
so a messenger of vengeance[d] will be sent to punish
him.[e]
[12]It's safer to meet a grizzly bear robbed of her cubs
than to confront a reckless fool.
[13]The one who returns evil for good
can expect to be treated the same way for the rest of
his life.[f]
[14]Don't be one who is quick to quarrel,

---

a 17:6 Or "fathers." There is an additional verse found in the Septuagint that is inserted here: "A whole world of riches belongs to the
faithful, but the unfaithful don't get even a cent."
b 17:7 Two absurd things are to find a fool in leadership and to have
a leader in foolishness.
c 17:8 "Instruction" is taken from the Aramaic and the Septuagint. The
Hebrew reads "bribe."
d 17:11 Or "merciless angels."
e 17:11 This could mean an evil spirit or calamities and sorrows.
f 17:13 Or "evil will haunt his house."

for an argument is hard to stop,
and you never know how it will end,
so don't even start down that road!^a

¹⁵There is nothing God hates more
than condemning the one who is innocent
and acquitting the one who is guilty.

¹⁶Why pay tuition to educate a fool?
For he has no intention of acquiring true wisdom.

¹⁷A dear friend will love you no matter what,
and a family sticks together through all kinds of
trouble.

¹⁸It's stupid to run up bills you'll never be able to pay
or to cosign for the loan of your friend.
Save yourself the trouble and don't do either one.

*Don't
gamble
debt*

¹⁹If you love to argue,
then you must be in love with sin.
For the one who loves to boast^b is only asking for
trouble.

²⁰The one with a perverse heart never has anything
good to say,^c
and the chronic liar tumbles into constant trouble.

²¹Parents of a numbskull will have many sorrows,
for there's nothing about his lifestyle that will make
them proud.

²²A joyful, cheerful heart brings healing to both body
and soul.
But the one whose heart is crushed
struggles with sickness and depression.

²³When you take a secret bribe,

---

a 17:14 The Aramaic for this verse reads "To shed blood provokes the judgment of a ruler."

b 17:19 Or "he who builds a high gate." The gate becomes a picture of the mouth. This is a figure of speech for proud boasting.

c 17:20 Or "can expect calamity."

your actions reveal your true character,
for you pervert the ways of justice.
²⁴Even the face of a wise man shows his intelligence.
But the wandering eyes of a fool will look for wisdom everywhere
except right in front of his nose.
²⁵A father grieves over the foolishness of his child,
and bitter sorrow fills his mother.
²⁶It's horrible to persecute a holy lover of God
or to strike an honorable man for his integrity!
²⁷Can you bridle your tongue when your heart is under
pressure?
That's how you show that you are wise.
An understanding heart keeps you cool, calm, and
collected,
no matter what you're facing.
²⁸When even a fool bites his tongue*ᵃ*
he's considered wise.
So shut your mouth when you are provoked—
it will make you look smart.

Wisdom Gives Life

18 An unfriendly person isolates himself
and seems to care only about his own issues.
For his contempt of sound judgment makes him a
recluse.*ᵇ*
²Senseless people find no pleasure in acquiring true
wisdom,
for all they want to do is impress you with what they
know.
³An ungodly man is always cloaked with disgrace,

---

a 17:28 The Septuagint is "When an unthinking man asks a question."
b 18:1 There are alternate possible translations of this verse in the Hebrew; for example, "An idle man meditates on his lusts and mocks wise instruction."

as dishonor and shame are his companions.
⁴Words of wisdom*a* are like a fresh, flowing brook—
  like deep waters that spring forth from within,
  bubbling up inside the one with understanding.
⁵It is atrocious when judges show favor to the guilty
  and deprive the innocent of justice.
⁶A senseless man jumps headfirst into an argument;
  he's just asking for a beating for his reckless words.*b*
⁷A fool has a big mouth that only gets him into trouble,
  and he'll pay the price for what he says.
⁸The words of a gossip merely reveal the wounds of
  his own soul,*c*
  and his slander penetrates into the innermost being.
⁹The one who is too lazy to look for work
  is the same one who wastes his life away.
¹⁰The character of God is a tower of strength,*d*
  for the lovers of God delight to run into his heart
  and be exalted on high.
¹¹The rich, in their conceit, imagine that their wealth
  is enough to protect them.
  It becomes their confidence in a day of trouble.*e*
¹²A man's heart is the proudest when his downfall is
  nearest,
  for he won't see glory until the Lord sees humility.
¹³Listen before you speak,

---

a 18:4 Or "Words that touch the heart."
b 18:6 The Aramaic is "his rash words call for death."
c 18:8 Scholars are somewhat uncertain about an exact translation of
  this phrase. The Aramaic is "The words of a lazy man lead him to
  fear and evil."
d 18:10 The Hebrew word *migdal*, translated as "tower of strength,"
  has a homonym that can be translated "bed of flowers."
e 18:11 The Aramaic is "The wealth of the rich is a strong city, and its
  glory casts a broad shadow."

for to speak before you've heard the facts will bring
humiliation.
[14]The will to live sustains you when you're sick,[a]
but depression crushes courage and leaves you
unable to cope.
[15]The spiritually hungry are always ready to learn
more,
for their hearts are eager to discover new truths.
[16]Would you like to meet a very important person?
Take a generous gift.
It will do wonders to gain entrance into his presence.
[17]There are two sides to every story.
The first one to speak sounds true until you hear the
other side
and they set the record straight.[b]
[18]A coin toss[c] resolves a dispute
and can put an argument to rest
between formidable opponents.
[19]It is easier to conquer a strong city
than to win back a friend whom you've offended.
Their walls go up, making it nearly impossible to
win them back.[d]
[20]Sharing words of wisdom is satisfying to your inner
being.
It encourages you to know
that you've changed someone else's life.[e]
[21]Your words are so powerful

---

a 18:14 The Septuagint is "A wise servant can calm a man's anger."

b 18:17 The text implies that a legal testimony in a courtroom may
seem to be correct until cross-examination begins.

c 18:18 The Hebrew is "Casting lots."

d 18:19 Or "A brother supported by a brother is like a high, strong city.
They hold each other up like the bars of a fortress."

e 18:20 Or "A man's belly is filled with the fruits of his mouth, and by
the harvest of his lips he will be satisfied."

that they will kill or give life,
and the talkative person will reap the consequences.
²²When a man finds a wife,
he has found a treasure!
For she is the gift of God to bring him joy and
pleasure.
But the one who divorces a good woman
loses what is good from his house.*ᵃ*
*To choose an adulteress is both stupid and ungodly.*ᵇ
²³The poor plead for help from the rich,
but all they get in return is a harsh response.
²⁴Some friendships don't last for long,ᶜ
but there is one loving friend who is joined to your
heartᵈ
closer than any other!

Wisdom Exalted

19 It's better to be honest, even if it leads to poverty,
than to live as a dishonest fool.

★ ²The best way to live is with revelation-knowledge,
for without it, you'll grow impatient and run right
into error.ᵉ
³There are some people who ruin their own lives
and then blame it all on God.
⁴Being wealthy means having lots of "friends,"
but the poor can't keep the ones they have.
⁵Perjury won't go unpunished,

---

a 18:22 The reference to divorce is not found in the Hebrew text but is
included in both the Aramaic and the Septuagint.

b 18:22 As translated from the Septuagint.

c 18:24 Or "A man with too many friends may be broken to pieces."

d 18:24 The Hebrew word used here can be translated "joined
together," "stick close," "to cleave," "to pursue," or "to overtake."

e 19:2 Or "sin."

It's not good to be poor
wisdom will keep you secure
But riches can lead to problems
w/o wisdom

and liars will get all that they deserve.
⁶Everyone wants to be close to the rich and famous,
but a generous person has all the friends he wants!
⁷When a man is poor, even his family has no use for
him.
How much more will his "friends" avoid him—
for though he begs for help, they won't respond.ᵃ
⁸Do yourself a favor and love wisdom.
Learn all you can,
then watch your life flourish and prosper!
⁹Tell lies and you're going to get caught,
and the habitual liar is doomed.
¹⁰It doesn't seem right when you see a fool
living in the lap of luxury
or a prideful servant ruling over princes.
¹¹An understanding person demonstrates patience,
for mercyᵇ means holding your tongue.
When you are insulted,
be quick to forgive and forget it,
for you are virtuous when you overlook an offense.
¹²The rage of a king is like the roar of a lion,
but his sweet favor is like a gentle, refreshing rain.
¹³A rebellious son breaks a father's heart,
and a nagging wife can drive you crazy!
¹⁴You can inherit houses and land from your parents,
but a goodᶜ wife only comes as a gracious gift from
God!
¹⁵Go ahead—be lazy and passive.

---

a 19:7 The Aramaic and the Septuagint add a sentence not found in
the Hebrew: "The one who is malicious with his words is not to be
trusted."

b 19:11 The word translated "mercy" (merciful) here is found only in
the Septuagint.

c 19:14 Literally "prudent" or "understanding" wife.

But you'll go hungry if you live that way.
¹⁶Honor God's holy instructions
   and life will go well for you.
   But if you despise his ways and choose your own
      plans,
   you will die.
¹⁷Every time you give to the poor you make a loan to
   the Lord.
   Don't worry—you'll be repaid in full for all the good
      you've done.
¹⁸Don't be afraid to discipline your children
   while they're still young enough to learn.
   Don't indulge your children or be swayed by their
      protests.
¹⁹A hot-tempered man has to pay the price for his
   anger.
   If you bail him out once,
      you'll do it a dozen times.^a
²⁰Listen well to wise counsel
   and be willing to learn from correction
   so that by the end of your life
   you'll be known for your wisdom.
²¹A person may have many ideas concerning God's
   plan for his life,
   but only the designs of God's purpose will succeed
      in the end.
²²A man is charming when he displays tender mercies
   to others.
   And a lover of God who is poor and promises
      nothing   *better poor & honest than rich*
                                & lying

---

a 19:19 There is an implication in the Hebrew that he will get into
legal trouble. An alternate translation of this verse could be "An evil-
minded man will be injured; if you rescue him, his anger will only
intensify."

Keep your promises!

is better than a rich liar who never keeps his
 promises.
²³When you live a life of abandoned love,
 surrendered before the awe of God,
 here's what you'll experience:
 Abundant life. Continual protection.*ᵃ*
 And complete satisfaction!
²⁴There are some people who pretend they're hurt—
 deadbeats who won't even work to feed themselves.*ᵇ*
²⁵If you punish the insolent who don't know any better,
 they will learn not to mock.
 But if you correct a wise man,
 he will grow even wiser.
²⁶Children who mistreat their parents
 are an embarrassment to their family and a public
 disgrace.
²⁷So listen, my child.
 Don't reject correction
 or you will certainly wander from the ways of truth.*ᶜ*
²⁸A corrupt witness makes a mockery of justice,
 for the wicked never play by the rules.*ᵈ*
²⁹Judgment is waiting for those who mock the truth,
 and foolish living invites a beating.

Are You Living Wisely?

20 A drunkard is obnoxious, loud, and argumentative;
 you're a fool to get intoxicated with strong drink.
²The rage of a king is like the roar of a lion.
 Do you really want to go and make him angry?

---

a 19:23 Or "You will not be remembered for evil."
b 19:24 Or "the lazy man buries his fork in his plate and won't even lift
 it to his mouth."
c 19:27 Or "Stop listening to instruction that contradicts what you
 know is truth."
d 19:28 Or "the heart of the wicked feeds on evil."

³A person of honor*ª* will put an argument to rest.
   Only the stupid want to pick a fight.
⁴If you're too lazy to plant seed,
   it's too bad when you have no harvest on which to
      feed.*ᵇ*
⁵A man of deep understanding will give good advice,
   drawing it out from the well within.
⁶Many will tell you they're your loyal friends,
   but who can find one who is truly trustworthy?*ᶜ*
⁷The lovers of God will walk in integrity,
   and their children are fortunate
   to have godly parents as their examples.
⁸A righteous king sits on his judgment seat.
   He scatters evil away from his kingdom
   by his wise discernment.
⁹Which one of us can truly say,
   "I am free from sin in my life,
   for my heart is clean and pure"?*ᵈ*
¹⁰Mark it down:
   God hates it when you demonstrate a double
      standard—
   one for "them" and one for "you."
¹¹All children show what they're really like by how they
   act.
   You can discern their character,
   whether they are pure or perverse.

---

a 20:3 Or "It is the glory of a man." It's better to keep a friend than to win a fight.
b 20:4 The Aramaic and the Septuagint read "Rebuke a lazy man and he still has no shame, yet watch him go beg at harvest time."
c 20:6 Or "A compassionate man is hard to find, but it's even harder to find one who is faithful."
d 20:9 The Hebrew word translated "clean" can also mean "perfect" or "holy." The word translated "pure" can also mean "clear," "bright," "shining," or "unmixed." Through God's grace, by the blood of Jesus, believers have been purified, made holy, and set free from our sins.

¹²Lovers of God have been given eyes to see
and ears to hear from God.
¹³If you spend all your time sleeping, you'll grow poor.
So wake up, sleepyhead! Don't sleep on the job.
And then there will be plenty of food on your table.
¹⁴The buyer says, as he haggles over the price,
"That's junk. It's worthless!"
Then he goes out and brags,
"Look at the great bargain I got!"
¹⁵You may have an abundance of wealth,
piles of gold and jewels,
but there is something of far greater worth:
speaking revelation-words of knowledge.
¹⁶Anyone stupid enough to guarantee a loan for a
stranger[a]
deserves to have his property held as security.
¹⁷What you obtain dishonestly may seem sweet at first,
but sooner or later you'll live to regret it.[b]
¹⁸If you solicit good advice, then your plans will
succeed.
So don't charge into battle without wisdom,
for wars are won by skillful strategy.
¹⁹A blabbermouth will reveal your secrets,
so stay away from people who can't keep their
mouths shut.[c]
²⁰If you despise your father or mother,
your life will flicker out like a lamp,
extinguished into the deepest darkness.
²¹If an inheritance is gained too early in life,
it will not be blessed in the end.

---

a 20:16 Some manuscripts have "a promiscuous woman."

b 20:17 Or "The bread of falsehood may taste sweet at first, but afterward you'll have a mouth full of gravel."

c 20:19 The Aramaic adds a line: "One who is faithful in spirit hides a matter."

²²Don't ever say, "I'm going to get even with them
   if it's the last thing I do!"
   Wrap God's grace around your heart
   and he will be the one to vindicate you.
²³The Lord hates double standards—
   that's hypocrisy at its worst!ᵃ
²⁴It is the Lord who directs your life,
   for each step you take is ordained by God
   to bring you closer to your destiny.
   So much of your life, then, remains a mystery!ᵇ
²⁵Be careful in making a rash promise before God,
   or you may be trapped by your vow and live to
      regret it.
²⁶A wise king is able to discern corruption
   and remove wickedness from his kingdom.ᶜ
²⁷The spirit God breathed into manᵈ is like a living lamp,
   a shining light
   searching into the innermost chamber of our being.
²⁸Good leadershipᵉ is built on love and truth,
   for kindness and integrity
   are what keep leaders in their position of trust.
²⁹We admire the young for their strength and beauty,
   but the dignity of the old is their wisdom.ᶠ
³⁰When you are punished severely, you learn your
   lesson well—
   for painful experiences do wonders to change your life.

---

a 20:23 Or "The Lord hates differing weights, and dishonest scales are
   wicked."
b 20:24 The Aramaic reads "So what man is capable of ordering his
   way?"
c 20:26 Or "A wise king winnows the wicked and turns his chariot
   wheel over them."
d 20:27 Implied by the Hebrew word *nishmat*, also used in Gen. 2:7.
e 20:28 Or "A king's throne."
f 20:29 Or "their gray hair."

God Is the Source of Wisdom

21 It's as easy for God to steer a king's heart[a] for his purposes
as it is for him to direct the course of a stream.[b]

[2]We may think we're right all the time,
but God thoroughly examines our motives.

[3]It pleases God more when we demonstrate godliness and justice
than when we merely offer him a sacrifice.

[4]Arrogance, superiority, and pride are the fruits of sin.[c]

[5]Brilliant ideas pay off and bring you prosperity,
but making hasty, impatient decisions
will only lead to financial loss.[d]

[6]You can make a fortune dishonestly,
but your crime will hold you in the snares of death![e]

[7]Violent rebels don't have a chance,
for their rejection of truth and their love of evil
will drag them deeper into darkness.

[8]You can discern that a person is guilty by his devious actions
and the innocence of a person by his honest, sincere ways.

---

a 21:1 Don't forget, we have been made kings and priests by the blood of the Lamb. See 1 Peter 2:9; Rev. 1:6; 5:10.

b 21:1 Because a leader's decisions affect so many people, God will intervene and steer them as a farmer steers the course of a stream to irrigate his fields.

c 21:4 Or "the tillage of the wicked." The Aramaic and the Septuagint have "the lamp of the wicked."

d 21:5 The Aramaic is "The thoughts of the chosen one are trusting, but those of the evil one lead to poverty." This verse is missing from the Septuagint.

e 21:6 As translated from the Aramaic and the Septuagint. The Hebrew is "the money will vanish into thin air."

⁹It's better to live all alone in a rickety shack
    than to share a castle with a crabby spouse!*a*
¹⁰The wicked always crave what is evil;
    they'll show no mercy and get no mercy.*b*
¹¹Senseless people learn their lessons the hard way,
    but the wise are teachable.
¹²A godly, righteous person*c* has the ability
    to bring the light of instruction to the wicked
    even though he despises what the wicked do.*d*
¹³If you close your heart to the cries of the poor,
    then I'll close my ears when you cry out to me!
¹⁴Try giving a secret gift to the one who is angry with
    you
    and watch his anger disappear.
    A kind, generous gift goes a long way
    to soothe the anger of one who is livid.*e*
¹⁵When justice is served,
    the lovers of God celebrate and rejoice,
    but the wicked begin to panic.
¹⁶When you forsake the ways of wisdom,
    you will wander into the realm of dark spirits.*f*

---

a 21:9 The Septuagint reads "It's better to live in the corner of an attic than in a large home plastered with unrighteousness."

b 21:10 The Hebrew is "they show no mercy," while the Septuagint reads "they'll receive no mercy." This translation merges both concepts.

c 21:12 The Hebrew is "a righteous one," which can also speak of God, "the Righteous One."

d 21:12 As translated from the Septuagint. There are many examples of this in the Bible: Joseph in Egypt, Daniel in Babylon, and the follower of Jesus today who is living among unbelievers.

e 21:14 The Aramaic and Septuagint translate this "He who withholds a gift arouses anger."

f 21:16 Or "the congregation of the Rephaites." The Rephaites were a pagan tribe of giants and have been equated with spirits of darkness. See Gen. 14:5 and Deut. 2:11.

¹⁷To love pleasure for pleasure's sake
   will introduce you to poverty.
   Indulging in a life of luxury^a
   will never make you wealthy.
¹⁸The wicked bring on themselves
   the very suffering they planned for others,
   for their treachery comes back to haunt them.^b
¹⁹It's better to live in a hut in the wilderness
   than with a crabby, scolding spouse!
²⁰In wisdom's house you'll find delightful treasures
   and the oil of the Holy Spirit.^c
   But the stupid^d squander what they've been given.
²¹The lovers of God who chase after righteousness
   will find all their dreams come true:
   an abundant life drenched with favor
   and a fountain that overflows with satisfaction.^e
²²A warrior filled with wisdom ascends into the high
   place
   and releases breakthrough,
   bringing down the strongholds of the mighty.^f
²³Watch your words and be careful what you say,
   and you'll be surprised by how few troubles you'll
   have.
²⁴An arrogant man is inflated with pride—
   nothing but a snooty scoffer in love with his own
   opinion.
   Mr. Mocker is his name!^g

---

a 21:17 Or "loving wine and oil."
b 21:18 Or "The evil become the ransom payment for the righteous
   and the faithless for the upright."
c 21:20 The Hebrew word for "oil" is an emblem of the Holy Spirit.
d 21:20 Or "a fool of a man."
e 21:21 Or "righteousness."
f 21:22 Or "demolishing their strength of confidence."
g 21:24 The Septuagint adds a line: "He who holds a grudge is a sinner."

²⁵⁻²⁶Taking the easy way out is the habit of a lazy man,
    and it will be his downfall.
    All day long he thinks about all the things that he
        craves,
    for he hasn't learned the secret that the generous
        man has learned:
    extravagant giving never leads to poverty.*ᵃ*
²⁷To bring an offering to God with an ulterior motive is
        detestable,
    for it amounts to nothing but hypocrisy.
²⁸No one believes a notorious liar,
    but the guarded words of an honest man stand the
        test of time.
²⁹The wicked are shameless and stubborn,
    but the lovers of God have a holy confidence.
³⁰All your brilliant wisdom and clever insight
    will be of no help at all if the Lord is against you.
³¹You can do your best to prepare for the battle,*ᵇ*
    but ultimate victory comes from the Lord God.

How to Live a Life of Wisdom

2 2 A beautiful reputation is more to be desired than
        great riches,*ᶜ*
    and to be esteemed by others is more honorable
        than to own immense investments.*ᵈ*
²The rich and the poor have one thing in common:
    the Lord God created each one.

---

a 21:25–26 This is implied in the context and is necessary to complete
    the meaning of the proverb. The last line of this verse in the Septu-
    agint reads "the righteous lavish on others mercy and compassion."
b 21:31 Or "The horse is prepared for the battle."
c 22:1 The Hebrew is simply "name preferred to wealth." The Aramaic
    indicates it could be "the name [of God]."
d 22:1 Or "silver and gold." Remember, it is Solomon, one of the rich-
    est men to ever live, who penned these words.

³A prudent person with insight foresees danger
coming
and prepares himself for it.ᵃ
But the senseless rush blindly forward
and suffer the consequences.

*Turn
r⁻/
over*

⁴Laying your life down in tender surrender before the
Lord
will bring life, prosperity, and honor as your reward.
⁵Twisted and perverse lives are surrounded by
demonic influence.ᵇ
If you value your soul, stay far away from them.
⁶Dedicate your children to God
and point them in the way that they should go,ᶜ
and the values they've learned from you will be with
them for life.
⁷If you borrow money with interest,
you'll end up serving the interests of your creditors,ᵈ
for the rich rule over the poor.
⁸Sin is a seed that brings a harvest;
you'll reap a heap of trouble with every seed you
plant.
For your investment in sins pays a full return—
the full punishment you deserve!ᵉ

---

a 22:3 Wise people solve problems before they happen.
b 22:5 Or "thorns and snares." This becomes a metaphor for demonic
   curses and troubles. Thorns are associated with the fall of Adam.
   Jesus wore a crown of thorns and took away our curse. The snares
   picture the temptations of evil that the devil places in our path.
c 22:6 Or "train them in the direction they are best suited to go." Some
   Jewish scholars teach this means understanding your children's tal-
   ents and then seeing that they go into that field.
d 22:7 The Septuagint reads "the servant will lend to his own master."
e 22:8 As translated from the Septuagint.

⁹When you are generous*a* to the poor,
   you are enriched with blessings in return.
¹⁰Say goodbye to a troublemaker and you'll say goodbye
   to quarrels, strife, tension, and arguments,
   for a troublemaker traffics in shame.*b*
¹¹The Lord loves those whose hearts are holy,
   and he is the friend of those whose ways are pure.*c*
¹²God passionately watches*d* over
   his deep reservoir*e* of revelation-knowledge,
   but he subverts the lies of those who pervert the truth.
¹³A slacker always has an excuse for not working—
   like "I can't go to work. There's a lion outside!
   And murderers too!"f
¹⁴Sex with an adulteress is like falling into the abyss.
   Those under God's curse jump right in to their own destruction.
¹⁵Although rebellion*g* is woven into a young man's heart,
   tough discipline can make him into a man.

---

a 22:9 The Hebrew word translated here as "generous" actually means "to have a bountiful eye." It is a figure of speech for generosity, a life of helping others.

b 22:10 As translated from the Aramaic.

c 22:11 As translated from the Septuagint. Followers of Jesus enjoy a relationship with our holy King as we live in the light and love to please him.

d 22:12 Or "the eyes of the Lord [watch]." In the church today, prophets become eyes in the body of Christ. They see and reveal God's heart for his people.

e 22:12 Although the concept of a reservoir is not found in the Hebrew, this translation adds it for poetic nuance.

f 22:13 This humorous verse uses both satire and a metaphor. There's always an excuse for not working hard. The Aramaic text adds "And murderers too!"

g 22:15 The Aramaic word used here means "senseless."

¹⁶There are two kinds of people headed toward
poverty:
those who exploit the poor
and those who bribe the rich.ᵃ

Sayings of the Wise Sages

¹⁷Listen carefully and open your heart.ᵇ
Drink in the wise revelation that I impart.
¹⁸You'll become winsome and wise
when you treasure the beauty of my words.
And always be prepared to share them at the appropriate time.
¹⁹For I'm releasing these words to you this day,
yes, even to you, so that your living hope
will be found in God alone,
for he is the only one who is always true.
²⁰⁻²¹Pay attention to these excellent sayings of three-
fold things.ᶜ
For within my words you will discover true and
reliable revelation.

---

a 22:16 The Hebrew is literally "Oppressing the poor is gain; giving to
the rich is loss. Both end up only in poverty."

b 22:17 From this verse to 24:22 we have a collection of proverbs that
lead to virtue. They are especially designed for the young person
about to enter a career and start a family.

c 22:20–21 As translated from the Aramaic. Most translators find
this verse difficult to convey. The Hebrew can be "I have written
excellent things," "I have written three times," "I write thirty sayings
[proverbs]," "I have written you previously," or "I have written you
generals." The Septuagint reads "You should copy these things three
times." If the Proverbs contain keys to understanding riddles and
mysteries (see Prov. 1:2–6), then we have one of those keys given to
us here. God speaks in threes, for he is a triune God. We have a body,
soul, and spirit. God lived in a three-room house (the outer court, the
Holy Place, and the chamber of the Most Holy Place). These three-
fold dimensions are throughout the Bible.

They will give you serenity*a* so that you can reveal
the truth of the word of the one who sends you.
²²Never oppress the poor
or pass laws with the motive of crushing the weak.
²³For the Lord will rise to plead their case
and humiliate the one who humiliates the poor.*b*
²⁴⁻²⁵Walk away from an angry man
or you'll embrace a snare in your soul*c*
by becoming bad-tempered just like him.
²⁶Why would you ever guarantee a loan for someone
else
or promise to be responsible for someone's debts?
²⁷For if you fail to pay you could lose your shirt!*d*
²⁸The previous generation has set boundaries in place.
Don't you dare move them just to benefit yourself.*e*
²⁹If you are uniquely gifted in your work,
you will rise and be promoted.
You won't be held back—
you'll stand before kings!

Wisdom Will Protect You

2 3 When you've been invited to dine with a very
important leader,
consider your manners and keep in mind whom
you're with.

---

a 22:20–21 *Serenity* is only found in the Aramaic.

b 22:23 As translated from the Aramaic. The Hebrew is "he will rob the soul of the one who robs the poor."

c 22:24–25 As translated from the Aramaic.

d 22:27 Or "bed."

e 22:28 This refers to moving property lines of your neighbors to take more land, or it could mean moving landmarks and memorials placed there by ancestors. It also speaks to the moral boundaries that the previous generation modeled—they are to be upheld.

²Be careful to curb your appetite and catch yourself
　　before you fall into the trap of wanting all you see.*a*
³Don't crave their delicacies,
　　for they may have another motive in having you sit
　　　at their table.
⁴Don't compare yourself to the rich.*b*
　　Surrender your selfish ambition and evaluate them
　　　properly.
⁵For no sooner do you start counting your wealth
　　than it sprouts wings and flies away like an eagle in
　　　the sky—
　　here today, gone tomorrow!
⁶Be sensible when you dine with a stingy man*c*
　　and don't eat more than you should.*d*
⁷For as he thinks within himself, so is he.*e*
　　He will grudgingly say, "Go ahead and eat all you
　　　want,"
　　but in his heart he resents the fact that he has to
　　　pay for your meal.
⁸You'll be sorry you ate anything at all,*f*
　　and all your compliments will be wasted.
⁹A rebellious fool will despise your wise advice,
　　so don't even waste your time—save your breath!

---

a 23:2 Or "put a knife to your throat." When you spend time with an
　important person, think about his needs, not your own, and favor
　will come on your life.

b 23:4 As translated from the Septuagint.

c 23:6 The Hebrew here literally means "an evil eye," which is a met-
　aphor for a stingy man.

d 23:6 Or "don't crave his delicacies."

e 23:7 The Aramaic, the Septuagint, and a few Hebrew manuscripts
　read "Eating with him is like eating with someone with a hair in his
　throat—his mind is not with you!"

f 23:8 Or "You'll vomit up the little you've eaten."

¹⁰Never move a long-standing boundary line
    or attempt to take land that belongs to the
      fatherless.
¹¹For they have a mighty protector,
    a loving redeemer,ᵃ who watches over them,
    and he will stand up for their cause.
¹²Pay close attention to the teaching that corrects you,
    and open your heart to every word of instruction.
¹³Don't withhold appropriate discipline from your
    child.
    Go ahead and punish him when he needs it.ᵇ
    Don't worry—it won't kill him!
¹⁴A good spanking could be the very thing
    that teaches him a lifelong lesson!ᶜ
¹⁵My beloved child, when your heart is full of wisdom,
    my heart is full of gladness.
¹⁶And when you speak anointed words,ᵈ
    we are speaking mouth to mouth!ᵉ
¹⁷Don't allow the actions of evil men
    to cause you to burn with anger.ᶠ
    Instead, burn with unrelenting passion
    as you worship God in holy awe.

---

a 23:11 The Hebrew word here is *goel*, which means "kinsman-redeemer." The Aramaic word means "Savior." This shows powerfully how God will take up the grievances of the oppressed.

b 23:13 The Hebrew is "strike them with the rod."

c 23:14 Or "rescues him from death." The Hebrew word is *Sheol.*

d 23:16 Or "speak what is right."

e 23:16 This is taken from the Septuagint, and it literally means "Your lips shall speak with my lips." The Hebrew is "My kidneys [soul] will rejoice." See Num. 12:6–8, which reveals that God spoke with Moses "mouth to mouth" (literal Hebrew).

f 23:17 The Hebrew word used here describes an emotion of intense passion. Many translate it "envy" ("Do not envy the sinner"), but that does not describe it fully. Another possible translation would be "zeal."

¹⁸Your future is bright and filled with a living hope
that will never fade away.
¹⁹As you listen to me, my beloved child,
you will grow in wisdom and your heart
will be drawn into understanding,
which will empower you to make right decisions.ᵃ
²⁰Don't live in the excesses of drunkenness or gluttony,
or waste your life away by partying all the time,ᵇ
²¹because drunkards and gluttons sleep their lives
away
and end up broke!
²²Give respect to your father and mother,
for without them you wouldn't even be here.
And don't neglect them when they grow old.
²³Embrace the truthᶜ and hold it close.
Don't let go of wisdom, instruction, and life-giving
understanding.
²⁴When a father observes his child living in godliness,
he is ecstatic with joy—nothing makes him prouder!
²⁵So may your father's heart burst with joy
and your mother's soul be filled with gladness
because of you.
²⁶My son, give me your heart
and embrace fully what I'm about to tell you.
²⁷Stay far away from prostitutes
and you'll stay far away from the pit of destruction.
For sleeping with a promiscuous woman is like falling into a trap
that you'll never be able to escape!

---

a 23:19 The Aramaic is "set up my doctrines in your heart."
b 23:20 Translated from the Aramaic and the Septuagint.
c 23:23 The Hebrew word here literally means "create the truth" or
"give birth to truth" or "possess the truth." This Hebrew word is also
used for God as the Creator. See Gen. 14:19, 22.

[28]Like a robber hiding in the shadows
   she's waiting to claim another victim—
   another husband unfaithful to his wife.
[29]Who has anguish? Who has bitter sorrow?
   Who constantly complains and argues?
   Who stumbles and falls and hurts himself?
   Who's the one with bloodshot eyes?
[30]It's the one who drinks too much
   and is always looking for a brew.
   Make sure it's never you!
[31]And don't be drunk with wine[a]
   but be known as one who enjoys the company
   of the lovers of God,[b]
[32]for drunkenness brings the sting of a serpent,
   like the fangs of a viper[c] spreading poison into your
      soul.
[33]It will make you hallucinate, mumble,
   and speak words that are perverse.
[34]You'll be like a seasick sailor being tossed to and fro,
   dizzy and out of your mind.
[35]You'll awake only to say, "What hit me?
   I feel like I've been run over by a truck!"
   Yet off you'll go, looking for another drink!

---

a 23:31 As translated from the Septuagint.
b 23:31 As translated from the Septuagint and a marginal reading of
   the Hebrew. The Aramaic is "Meditate on righteousness." The Septuagint adds a line not found in Hebrew or Aramaic that describes
   the unflattering life of a drunk: "You will walk around naked as a
   pestle!"
c 23:32 Or "horned serpent" or "dragon." This is an emblem of the
   poison of demonic power that can cause addictions and rule over
   the soul.

Wisdom's Warning

24 Don't envy the wealth of the wicked or crave their company.

²For they're obsessed with causing trouble
and their conversations are corrupt.
³Wise people are builders*ᵃ*—
they build families, businesses, communities.
And through intelligence and insight
their enterprises are established and endure.
⁴Because of their skilled leadership,
the hearts*ᵇ* of people are filled with the treasures of
wisdom
and the pleasures of spiritual wealth.
⁵Wisdom can make anyone into a mighty warrior,*ᶜ*
and revelation-knowledge increases strength.
⁶Wise strategy is necessary to wage war,
and with many astute advisers
you'll see the path to victory more clearly.
⁷Wisdom is a treasure too lofty for a quarreling fool*ᵈ*—
he'll have nothing to say when leaders gather
together.
⁸There is one who makes plans to do evil—
Master Schemer is his name.
⁹If you plan to do evil, it's as wrong as doing it.
And everyone detests a troublemaker.

---

a 24:3 Or "A house is built by wisdom." The house is more than a structure with roof and a floor. It becomes a metaphor for families, churches, businesses, and enterprises.
b 24:4 Or "inner chambers."
c 24:5 Or "Wisdom makes anyone into a hero." The Aramaic and the Septuagint read "It's better to be wise than to be strong."
d 24:7 The Hebrew is actually "Wisdom is coral to a fool." That is, it is unattainable, deep, and hidden.

¹⁰If you faint when under pressure,
  you have need of courage.*
¹¹Go and rescue the perishing! Be their savior!
  Why would you stand back and watch them stagger
    to their death?
¹²And why would you say, "But it's none of my
business"?
  The one who knows you completely and judges your
    every motive
  is also the keeper of souls—and not just yours!
  He sees through your excuses and holds you
    responsible
  for failing to help those whose lives are threatened.
¹³Revelation-knowledge is a delicacy,
  sweet like flowing honey that melts in your mouth.
  Eat as much of it as you can, my friend!
¹⁴For then you will perceive what is true wisdom,
  your future will be bright,*
  and this hope living within you will never disappoint
    you.
¹⁵Listen up, you wicked, irreverent ones—
  don't harass the lovers of God*
  and don't invade their resting place.
¹⁶For the lovers of God may suffer adversity
  and stumble seven times,
  but they will continue to rise over and over again.

---

a 24:10 Or "your strength is limited." Our weakness often becomes
an excuse to quit, but strength and courage come as the result of
faithfulness under pressure. Some interpret this to mean "If you fail
to help others in their time of need, you will grow too weak to help
yourself."
b 24:14 The Septuagint is "your death will be good."
c 24:15 Or "the righteous."

But the unrighteous are brought down by just one
calamity
and will never be able to rise again.[a]
[17]Never gloat when your enemy meets disaster,
and don't be quick to rejoice if he falls.
[18]For the Lord, who sees your heart,
will be displeased with you and will pity your foe.
[19]Don't be angrily offended over evildoers or be agitated by them.[b]
[20]For the wicked have no life and no future—
their light of life will die out.[c]
[21]My child, stand in awe of Yahweh!
Give counsel to others,
but don't mingle with those who are rebellious.
[22]For sudden destruction will fall upon them
and their lives will be ruined in a moment.
And who knows what retribution they will face![d]

Revelation from the Wise

[23]Those enlightened with wisdom have spoken these
proverbs:
Judgment must be impartial,
for it is always wrong to be swayed by a person's
status.
[24]If you say to the guilty, "You are innocent,"
the nation will curse you and the people will revile
you.
[25]But when you convict the guilty,
the people will thank you and reward you with favor.

---

a 24:16 Implied in the text, as it completes the parallelism.
b 24:19 The Septuagint is "Don't rejoice with those who do evil or be jealous of them."
c 24:20 Not only will they die out, but the implication is they will also have no posterity.
d 24:22 Verses 21 and 22 are translated from the Aramaic.

[26]Speaking honestly is a sign of true friendship.[a]
[27]Go ahead, build your career and give yourself to your
work.
But if you put me first, you'll see your family built up![b]
[28]Why would you be a false accuser and slander with
your words?
[29]Don't ever spitefully say, "I'll get even with him!
I'll do to him what he did to me!"
[30-31]One day I passed by the field of a lazy man,
and I noticed the vineyards of a slacker.
I observed nothing but thorns, weeds, and broken-
down walls.
[32]So I considered their lack of wisdom,
and I pondered the lessons I could learn from this:
[33-34]Professional work habits prevent poverty from
becoming
your permanent business partner. And:
If you put off until tomorrow the work you could do
today,
tomorrow never seems to come.

2 5 Solomon's proverbs, published by the scribes
of King Hezekiah:
[2]God conceals the revelation of his word[c]
in the hiding place of his glory.[d]

---

a 24:26 The Hebrew is literally "An honest answer is like a kiss on
the lips." In the culture of the day, kissing was a sign of authentic
friendship and a mark of relationship, which was often expressed in
public among friends.
b 24:27 As translated from the Septuagint.
c 25:2 Many translate this "a matter," whereas the Hebrew is *dabar*,
which is translated more than eight hundred times in the Old Testament as "word."
d 25:2 There is beautiful poetry in the Hebrew text. The word for
"hide" is *cathar*, and the word for "word" is *dabar*. The Hebrew is
actually "*Kabod* [glory] *cathar* [hidden] *dabar* [word]."

But the honor of kings[a] is revealed
by how they thoroughly search out
the deeper meaning of all that God says.
³The heart of a king is full of understanding,
like the heavens are high and the ocean is deep.
⁴If you burn away the impurities from silver,
a sterling vessel will emerge from the fire.
⁵And if you purge corruption from the kingdom,
a king's reign will be established in righteousness.
⁶Don't boast in the presence of a king
or promote yourself by taking a seat at the head
table
and pretending that you're someone important.
⁷For it is better for the king to say to you,
"Come, you should sit at the head table,"
than for him to say in front of everyone,
"Please get up and move—
you're sitting in the place of the prince."
⁸Don't be hasty to file a lawsuit.
By starting something you wish you hadn't,
you could be humiliated when you lose your case.
⁹Don't reveal another person's secret
just to prove a point in an argument,
or you could be accused of being a gossip
¹⁰and gain a reputation for being one
who betrays the confidence of a friend.
¹¹Winsome words spoken at just the right time
are as appealing as apples gilded in gold

---

a 25:2 We have been made kings and priests, royal lovers of God,
because of God's grace and Christ's redeeming blood. See 1 Peter
2:9 and Rev. 5:8–10.

surrounded with silver.[a]

[12]When you humbly receive wise correction,
it adorns your life with beauty[b]
and makes you a better person.

[13]A reliable, trustworthy messenger
refreshes the heart of his master,[c]
like a gentle snowfall at harvest time.

[14]Clouds that carry no water
and a wind that brings no refreshing rain[d]—
that's what you're like when you boast
of a gift that you don't have.[e]

Wisdom Practices Self-Control

[15]Use patience and kindness when you want to per-
suade leaders
and watch them change their minds right in front of
you.

---

a 25:11 The Aramaic reads "The one who speaks the word is an apple
of gold in a setting of silver." The Septuagint is "A wise word is like
a golden apple in a pendant of rubies." Each one of God's promises
are like apples gilded in gold. When we are full of his Spirit, we can
speak and prophesy words of encouragement that are spoken at the
right time for the blessing of others.

b 25:12 Or "an earring of gold, an ornament of fine gold." An earring
pierces the ear and is an emblem of a listening heart.

c 25:13 Or "employer."

d 25:14 The symbols of clouds, wind, and rain are significant. Clouds
are often a metaphor for the people of God filled with glory (see Heb.
12:1; Rev. 1:7). Wind is an emblem of the Holy Spirit bringing new
life (see John 3:6–8). Rain often points to teaching the revelation-
truths that refresh and water the seeds of spiritual growth (see Isa.
55:10–11). God's anointed people are to be clouds carried by the
wind of the Holy Spirit that bring refreshing truths to his people.
When we are empty and false, we are clouds without rain. See also
2 Peter 2:17 and Judah (Jude) 12.

e 25:14 Or "boast of a promised gift you never intend to give." The
Hebrew is literally "to make yourself shine in a gift of falsehood."

For your gentle wisdom will quell the strongest
  resistance.[a]
[16]When you discover something sweet,
  don't overindulge and eat more than you need,
  for excess in anything can make you sick of even a
    good thing.
[17]Don't wear out your welcome
  by staying too long at the home of your friends,
  or they may get fed up with always having you there
  and wish you hadn't come.
[18]Lying about and slandering people
  are as bad as hitting them with a club,
  or wounding them with an arrow,
  or stabbing them with a sword.
[19]You can't depend on an unreliable person
  when you really need help.
  It can be compared to biting down on an abscessed
    tooth
  or walking with a sprained ankle.
[20]When you sing a song of joy to someone suffering
  in the deepest grief and heartache,
  it can be compared to disrobing in the middle of a
    blizzard
  or rubbing salt in a wound.
[21]Is your enemy hungry? Buy him lunch.[b]
  Win him over with your kindness.
[22]Your surprising generosity will awaken his
  conscience[c]
  and God will reward you with favor.
[23]As the north wind brings a storm,

---

a 25:15 Or "Soft words break bones."
b 25:21 Or "Is he thirsty? Give him a drink."
c 25:22 Or "You will heap coals of fire on his head." His heart will be
  moved and his shame exposed.

saying things you shouldn't[a] brings a storm to any
    relationship.
[24]It's better to live all alone in a rundown shack
    than to share a castle with a crabby spouse![b]
[25]Like a drink of cool water refreshes a weary, thirsty
    soul,
    so hearing good news revives the spirit.
[26]When a lover of God gives in and compromises with
    wickedness,
        it can be compared to contaminating a stream with
            sewage
        or polluting a fountain.
[27]It's good to eat sweet things,
    but you can take too much.
    It's good to be honored,
    but to seek words of praise[c] is not honor at all.
[28]If you live without restraint
    and are unable to control your temper,
    you're as helpless as a city with broken-down defenses,
    open to attack.

Don't Be a Fool

26 It is totally out of place to promote and honor a
    fool,
        just like it's out of place to have snow in the summer
        and rain at harvest time.[d]
[2]An undeserved curse will be powerless to harm you.

---

a 25:23 Or "words of gossip."
b 25:24 With the exception of one Hebrew letter, this verse is identical
    to 21:9. See footnote. The Aramaic reads "than to live with a conten-
    tious woman in a house of divisions."
c 25:27 This line is translated from the Aramaic.
d 26:1 Both snow and rain are good in their proper season but harm-
    ful in the wrong season. So is it harmful to the fool if you promote
    and honor him prematurely.

It may flutter over you like a bird,
but it will find no place to land.ᵃ

³Guide a horse with a whip,
direct a donkey with a bridle,
and lead a rebellious fool with a beating on his
backside!

⁴Don't respond to the words of a fool with more foolish words,
or you will become as foolish as he is!

⁵Instead, if you're asked a silly question,
answer it with words of wisdomᵇ
so the fool doesn't think he's so clever.

⁶If you choose a fool to represent you,
you're asking for trouble.
It will be as bad for you as cutting off your own feet!

⁷You can never trust the words of a fool,
just like a crippled man can't trust his legs to support him.ᶜ

⁸Give honor to a fool and watch it backfire—
like a stone tied to a slingshot.

⁹The statements of a fool will hurt othersᵈ
like a thorn bush brandished by a drunk.

¹⁰Like a reckless archer shooting arrows at random
is the impatient employer
who hires just any fool who comes along—
someone's going to get hurt!ᵉ

---

a 26:2 There is an implication in some Hebrew manuscripts that the
curse will go back and land on the one who wrongly spoke it, like a
bird going back to its nest.

b 26:5 As translated from the Aramaic.

c 26:7 As translated from the Aramaic.

d 26:9 As translated from the Aramaic.

e 26:10 Implied in the context. This is a difficult verse to translate, and it
reads quite differently in the Aramaic and the Septuagint. The Aramaic
is "A fool suffers much, like a drunkard crossing the sea." The Septuagint
reads "Every fool endures much hardship and his fury comes to nothing."

¹¹Fools are famous for repeating their errors,
  like dogs are known to return to their vomit.
¹²There's only one thing worse than a fool,
  and that's the smug, conceited man
  always in love with his own opinions.

Don't Be Lazy
¹³The lazy loafer says,
  "I can't go out and look for a job—
  there may be a lion out there roaming wild in the
    streets!"
¹⁴As a door is hinged to the wall,
  so the lazy man keeps turning over, hinged to his
    bed!
¹⁵There are some people so lazy
  they won't even work to feed themselves.
¹⁶A self-righteous person[a] is convinced he's smarter
  than seven wise counselors who tell him the truth.
¹⁷It's better to grab a stray dog by its ears
  than to meddle in a quarrel[b]
  that's none of your business.

Watch Your Words
^{18–19}The one who is caught lying to his friend,
  who says, "I didn't mean it, I was only joking,"
  can be compared to a madman
  randomly shooting off deadly weapons.
²⁰It takes fuel to have a fire—
  a fire dies down when you run out of fuel.
  So quarrels disappear when the gossip ends.

---

a 26:16 Or "sluggard." This speaks of a person who lives in fantasy
  and not reality.
b 26:17 Or "to become furious because of a quarrel that's not yours."

²¹Add fuel to the fire and the blaze goes on.
    So add an argumentative man to the mix,
    and you'll keep strife alive.
²²Gossip is so delicious, and how we love to swallow it!
    For slander*a* is easily absorbed into our innermost
        being.
²³Smooth talk*b* can hide a corrupt heart
    just like a pretty glaze covers a cheap clay pot.
²⁴Kind words can be a cover to conceal hatred of
    others,
    for hypocrisy loves to hide behind flattery.
²⁵So don't be drawn in by the hypocrite,
    for his gracious speech is a charade,
    nothing but a masquerade covering his hatred and
        evil on parade.*c*
²⁶Don't worry—he can't keep the mask on for long.
    One day his hypocrisy will be exposed before all the
        world.
²⁷Go ahead, set a trap for others—
    and then watch as it snaps back on you!
    Start a landslide and you'll be the one who gets
        crushed.
²⁸Hatred is the root of slander*d*
    and insecurity the root of flattery.*e*

---

a 26:22 Or "complaining."
b 26:23 As translated from the Septuagint. The Hebrew is "Burning words."
c 26:25 The Hebrew is "seven abominations hide in his heart." This is a figure of speech for the fullness of evil, a heart filled to the brim with darkness.
d 26:28 Or "A slanderer hates his victims."
e 26:28 Or "A flattering mouth works ruin." The Aramaic is "Malicious words work trouble."

Heed Wisdom's Warnings

27 Never brag about the plans you have for tomorrow,
   for you don't have a clue what tomorrow may bring to you.
²Let someone else honor you for your accomplishments,
   for self-praise is never appropriate.
³It's easier to carry a heavy boulder and a ton of sand
   than to be provoked by a fool and have to carry that burden!
⁴The rage and anger of others can be overwhelming,
   but it's nothing compared to jealousy's fire.
⁵It's better to be corrected openly
   if it stems from hidden love.
⁶You can trust a friend who wounds you with his honesty,ᵃ
   but your enemy's pretended flatteryᵇ comes from insincerity.
⁷When your soul is full, you turn down even the sweetest honey.
   But when your soul is starving,
   every bitter thing becomes sweet.ᶜ
⁸Like a bird that has fallen from its nest
   is the one who is dislodged from his home.ᵈ
⁹Sweet friendshipsᵉ refresh the soul and awaken our hearts with joy,

---

a 27:6 Or "Amen [effective and faithful] are the wounds of love." This could be a reference to the wounds Jesus endured because of his love for us.

b 27:6 Or "kisses."

c 27:7 When we are full of many things and many opinions, the sweet word of God, like revelation honey, is spurned. Instead, we eat and fill our souls with things that can never satisfy.

d 27:8 Or "banished from his place," as translated from the Aramaic.

e 27:9 Or "counsel."

for good friends are like the anointing oil
that yields the fragrant incense *of God's presence.*[a]
[10]So never give up on a friend or abandon a friend of
your father—
for in the day of your brokenness[b]
you won't have to run to a relative for help.
A friend nearby is better than a relative far away.
[11]My son, when you walk in wisdom,
my heart is filled with gladness,
for the way you live is proof
that I've not taught you in vain.[c]
[12]A wise, shrewd person discerns the danger ahead
and prepares himself,
but the naïve simpleton never looks ahead
and suffers the consequences.
[13]Cosign for one you barely know and you will pay a
great price!
Anyone stupid enough to guarantee the loan of
another
deserves to have his property seized in payment.
[14]Do you think you're blessing your neighbors
when you sing at the top of your lungs early in the
morning?
Don't be fooled—
they'll curse you for doing it![d]
[15]An endless drip, drip, drip, from a leaky faucet[e]

---

a 27:9 The Hebrew text refers to the sacred anointing oil and the
incense that burns in the Holy Place.
b 27:10 As translated from the Aramaic.
c 27:11 Or "that I may answer those who reproach me."
d 27:14 Or "He who sings in a loud voice early in the morning, thinking he's blessing his neighbor, is no different from he who pro-
nounces a curse."
e 27:15 Or "a constant drip on a rainy day."

and the words of a cranky, nagging wife have the
  same effect.
¹⁶Can you stop the north wind from blowing
  or grasp a handful of oil?
  That's easier than to stop her from complaining.
¹⁷It takes a grinding wheel to sharpen a blade,
  and so one person sharpens the character of
    another.
¹⁸Tend an orchard and you'll have fruit to eat.
  Serve the Master's interests
  and you'll receive honor that's sweet.
¹⁹Just as no two faces are exactly alike,
  so every heart is different.[a]
²⁰Death and destruction are never filled,
  and the desires of men's hearts are insatiable.
²¹Fire is the way to test the purity of silver and gold,
  but the character of a man is tested
  by giving him a measure of fame.[b]
²²You can beat a fool half to death
  and still never beat the foolishness out of him.[c]
²³A shepherd should pay close attention to the faces of
  his flock
  and hold close to his heart the condition of those he
    cares for.
²⁴A man's strength, power, and riches[d] will one day
  fade away;
  not even nations[e] endure forever.

---

a 27:19 As translated from the Aramaic and the Septuagint.
b 27:21 Or "by the things he praises."
c 27:22 Or "If you pound a fool in a mortar with a pestle like dried
grain, still his foolishness will not depart from him."
d 27:24 The Hebrew says merely "riches," while the Aramaic adds
"power [dominion]" and the Septuagint adds "strength." This translation combines them.
e 27:24 Or "a crown" or "diadem [dominion]."

²⁵⁻²⁷Take care of your responsibilities
and be diligent in your business
and you will have more than enough—
an abundance of food, clothing, and plenty for your
household.ᵃ

Lovers of God

2 8 Guilty criminals experience paranoia
even though no one threatens them.
But the innocent lovers of God,
because of righteousness,
will have the boldnessᵇ of a young, ferocious lion!
²A rebellious nation is thrown into chaos,ᶜ
but leaders anointed with wisdom will restore law
and order.
³When a pauperᵈ oppresses the destitute,
it's like a flash flood that sweeps away their last
hope.
⁴Those who turn their backs on what they know is
rightᵉ
will no longer be able to tell right from wrong.
But those who love the truth strengthen their souls.ᶠ

---

a 27:25–27 An agricultural analogy is used in the Hebrew and Aramaic. The analogy of a farming enterprise has been changed to
business here in order to transfer meaning. It is literally "Gather the
hay of the field and hills, and new grass will appear. Lambs will pro-
vide clothing, goats will pay for the price of the field, and there will
be enough goat's milk for you, your family, and your servant girls."

b 28:1 Or "confidence."

c 28:2 Or "A rebellious nation will have one leader after another."

d 28:3 This pauper can also be one who is spiritually poor. Some Jewish expositors believe it refers to corrupt judges.

e 28:4 The Hebrew word is "the Torah." See vv. 7, 9.

f 28:4 As translated from the Aramaic. The Septuagint is "build a wall
to protect themselves."

⁵Justice never makes sense to men devoted to
  darkness,
    but those tenderly devoted to the Lord
    can understand justice perfectly.
⁶It's more respectable to be poor and pure than rich
  and perverse.
⁷To be obedient to what you've been taught*
  proves you're an honorable child,
    but to socialize with the lawless brings shame to
    your parents.
⁸Go ahead and get rich on the backs of the poor,
    but all the wealth you gather will one day be given
    to those who are kind to the needy.
⁹If you close your heart and refuse to listen to God's
  instruction,*
    even your prayer will be despised.
¹⁰Those who tempt the lovers of God with an evil
  scheme
    will fall into their own traps.
    But the innocent who resist temptation will experi-
    ence reward.
¹¹The wealthy in their conceit presume to be wise,
    but a poor person with discernment can see right
    through them.
¹²The triumphant joy of God's lovers releases great
  glory.*
    But when the wicked rise to power, everyone goes
    into hiding.*
¹³If you cover up your sin you'll never do well.
    But if you confess your sins and forsake them,
    you will be kissed by mercy.

---

a 28:7 Or "the Torah."
b 28:9 Or "the Torah."
c 28:12 As translated from the Aramaic.
d 28:12 Or "people become victims."

¹⁴Overjoyed is the one who with tender heart trembles
before God,
but the stubborn, unyielding heart will experience
even greater evil.
¹⁵Ruthless rulers can only be compared
to raging lions and roaming bears.*ᵃ*
¹⁶Abusive leaders fail to employ wisdom,
but leaders who despise corruption*ᵇ*
will enjoy a long and full life.*ᶜ*
¹⁷A murderer's conscience will torment him—
a fugitive haunted by guilt all the way to the grave
with no one to support him.
¹⁸The pure will be rescued from failure,
but the perverse will suddenly fall into ruin.
¹⁹Work hard and you'll have all you desire,
but chase a fantasy*ᵈ* and you could end up with
nothing.
²⁰Life's blessings drench the honest and faithful
person,
but punishment rains down upon the greedy and
dishonest.
²¹Giving favoritism to the rich and powerful is
disgusting,
and this is done by the type of judge who would
betray a man for a bribe.*ᵉ*

---

a 28:15 David, before he killed Goliath, went after the lion and the
bear. See 1 Sam. 17:34–37. These beasts represented demonic forces
of evil over the land. Daniel also mentions the world's ruthless leaders as lions and bears. See Dan. 7:1–8.
b 28:16 Or "injustice."
c 28:16 Or "enjoy a long reign."
d 28:19 Or "an empty dream." The Septuagint is "the one who pursues
leisure."
e 28:21 As translated from the Aramaic.

²²A greedy man[a] is in a race to get rich,
  but he forgets that he could lose what's most important
  and end up with nothing.[b]
²³If you correct someone with constructive criticism,
  in the end he will appreciate it more than flattery.
²⁴A person who would reject his own parents[c] and say,
  "What's wrong with that?" is as bad as a murderer.
²⁵To make rash, hasty decisions
  shows that you are not trusting the Lord.
  But when you rely totally on God,
  you will still act carefully and prudently.[d]
²⁶Self-confident know-it-alls[e] will prove to be fools.
  But when you lean on the wisdom from above,
  you will have a way to escape the troubles of your
    own making.
²⁷You will never go without if you give to the poor.
  But if you're heartless, stingy, and selfish,[f]
  you invite curses upon yourself.
²⁸When wicked leaders rise to power,
  good people go into hiding.
  But when they fall from power,
  the godly take their place.

---

a 28:22 Both the Aramaic and Hebrew have "The man with an evil eye." This is a figure of speech for a stingy or greedy man. A person who shuts his heart to the poor is said to have an evil eye. A person with a good eye is someone who looks on the poor with generosity.

b 28:22 As translated from the Aramaic. The Aramaic text sounds very similar to what Jesus says about gaining the world but losing our souls. See Mark 8:36.

c 28:24 As translated from the Septuagint. The Hebrew is "the one who steals from his own parents."

d 28:25 As translated from the Septuagint. The Hebrew is "The greedy person stirs up trouble, but the one who trusts in the Lord will prosper."

e 28:26 Or "those who trust their instincts."

f 28:27 Or "if you hide your eyes from the poor."

Don't Be Stubborn

2 9 Stubborn people who repeatedly refuse to accept correction
will suddenly be broken and never recover.
[2]Everyone rejoices when the lovers of God flourish,
but the people groan when the wicked rise to power.
[3]When you love wisdom, your father is overjoyed.
But when you associate with prostitutes,
you waste your wealth in exchange for disgrace.[a]
[4]A godly leader who values justice
is a great strength and example to the people.
But the one who sells his influence for money
tears down what is right.[b]
[5]Flattery can often be used as a trap to hide ulterior motives
and take advantage of you.
[6]The wicked always have a trap laid for others,
but the lovers of God escape as they sing and shout
in joyous triumph!
[7]God's righteous people will pour themselves out for
the poor,[c]
but the ungodly make no attempt to understand or
help the needy.

You Can't Argue with a Fool

[8]Arrogant cynics love to pick fights,
but the humble and wise love to pursue peace.
[9]There's no use arguing with a fool,[d]
for his ranting and raving prevent you from making
a case

---

a 29:3 See Luke 15:11–24.

b 29:4 See 1 Tim. 6:10.

c 29:7 The Hebrew text implies standing up for the legal rights of the poor.

d 29:9 The Hebrew implies an argument in a court of law.

and settling the argument in a calm way.

¹⁰Violent men hate those with integrity,
    but the lovers of God esteem those who are holy.ᵃ

¹¹You can recognize fools by the way
    they give full vent to their rage
    and let their words fly!
    But the wise bite their tongues and hold back all
        they could say.

¹²When leaders listen to false accusations,
    their associates become scoundrels.

¹³Poor people and their oppressors
    have only one thing in common—
    God made them both.ᵇ

¹⁴The best insurance for a leader's longevity
    is to demonstrate justice for the poor.

¹⁵Experiencing many corrections and rebukes will
    make you wise.
    But if left to your own ways, you'll bring disgrace to
        your parents.ᶜ

¹⁶When the wicked are in power, lawlessness abounds.
    But the patient lovers of God will one day watch in
        triumph
    as their stronghold topples!

¹⁷Correct your child and one day you'll find he has
    changed
    and will bring you great delight.

---

a 29:10 As translated from the Septuagint.
b 29:13 A figure of speech in Hebrew that can literally be translated
    "God gave them both the gift of eyesight." The Septuagint is "The
    contracts between lenders and debtors are observed by the Lord."
c 29:15 As translated from the Septuagint. The Hebrew is "your
    mother."

¹⁸When there is no clear prophetic vision,ᵃ
people quickly wander astray.ᵇ
But when you follow the revelation of the Word,
heaven's bliss fills your soul.
¹⁹A stubborn servant can't be corrected by words
alone.
For even if he understands, he pays no attention to
you.
²⁰There's only one kind of person who is worse than a
fool:
the impetuous one who speaks without thinking
first.
²¹If you pamper your servants,
don't be surprised when they expect to be treated as
sons.ᶜ
²²The source of strife is found in an angry heart,
for sin surrounds the life of a furious man.ᵈ
²³Lift yourself up with pride and you will soon be
brought low,ᵉ
but a meek and humble spirit will add to your
honor.

---

a 29:18 The Hebrew word used here can refer to a "vision of the night," "dream," "oracle," or "revelation." The Septuagint reads "where there is no prophetic seer [or interpreter]."

b 29:18 Or "let loose," "strip," or "made themselves naked." The Septuagint reads "the people become lawless."

c 29:21 Or "If you pamper your servant when he is young, he'll become a weakling in the end." The Septuagint reads "If you live in luxury as a child, you'll become a domestic [servant] and at last will be grieved with yourself." The Aramaic states, "You'll be uprooted in the end."

d 29:22 The Hebrew word translated as "a furious man" can also mean "lord of fury" or "Baal of wrath."

e 29:23 Or "to depression."

²⁴You are your own worst enemy when you partner
   with a thief,
   for a curse of guilt will come upon you
   when you fail to report a crime.ᵃ
²⁵Fear and intimidation is a trap that holds you back.
   But when you place your confidence in the Lord,
   you will be seated in the high place.
²⁶Everyone curries favor with leaders.
   But God is the judge, and justice comes from him.
²⁷The wicked hate those who live a godly life,
   but the righteous hate injustice wherever it's found.

The Mysterious Sayings of Agur

30 These are the collected sayings of the prophet
   Agur, Jakeh's sonᵇ—
   the amazing revelationᶜ he imparted to Ithiel and
   Ukal.ᵈ

---

a 29:24 Or "when under oath to testify but you do not talk."

b 30:1 This section of Proverbs is attributed to Agur, who gave these
   oracles to his protégés Ithiel and Ukal. Agur means "to gather a harvest." He was the son of Jakeh, which means "blameless" or "obedient." Jakeh could be another name for David, Solomon's father.
   Many Jewish expositors believe that Agur was a pseudonym for
   Solomon. Nothing more is mentioned about Agur in the Bible than
   what we have here, which is typical for other prophets mentioned in
   the Scriptures. Some believe he could be the "master of the collection of sayings" referred to in Eccl. 12:11.

c 30:1 Or "mighty prophecy."

d 30:1 The name Ithiel can mean "God is with me" or "God has arrived."
   This was fulfilled by Christ, for his birth was the advent, the arrival
   of God to the earth in human form. Ukal means "I am able" or "I
   am strong and mighty." When placed together, the meaning of these
   Hebrew names could read "Gather a harvest of sons who are blameless and obedient. They will have God with them, and they will be
   strong and mighty." This chapter contains some of the most mystical
   and mysterious sayings found in Proverbs, with hints of revelation
   from the book of Job.

²God, I'm so weary and worn out,
    I feel more like a beast than a man.
    I was made in your image,[a]
    but I lack understanding.
³I've yet to learn the wisdom
    that comes from the full and intimate knowledge of
        you,
    the Holy One.

Six Questions

⁴Who is it that travels back and forth
    from the heavenly realm to the earth?[b]
    Who controls the wind[c] as it blows and holds it in
        his fists?
    Who tucks the rain into the cloak of his clouds?
    Who stretches out the skyline from one vista to the
        other?
    What is his name?
    And what is the name of his Son?
    Who can tell me?

A Pure Heart Is Filled with God's Word

⁵Every promise from the faithful God
    is pure and proves to be true.
    He is a wraparound shield of protection for all his
        lovers
    who run to hide in him.

---

a 30:2 Implied in the text, which is extraordinarily difficult to translate
with certainty.

b 30:4 Jesus solves this riddle in John 3:13. Only Jesus Christ is the
master of heavenly knowledge and wisdom. See also Eph. 4:7–10.

c 30:4 The Hebrew word *ruach* (wind) is also the term used for the
Holy Spirit.

⁶Never add to his words,
  or he will have to rebuke you and prove that you're
    a liar.
⁷God, there are two things I'm asking you for before I
  die, only two:
⁸Empty out of my heart everything that is false—
  every lie, and every crooked thing.
  And give me neither undue poverty nor undue
    wealth—
  but rather, feed my soul with the measure of
    prosperity
  that pleases you.
⁹May my satisfaction be found in you.
  Don't let me be so rich that I don't need you
  or so poor that I have to resort to dishonesty
  just to make ends meet.
  Then my life will never detract from bringing glory
    to your name.
¹⁰Never defame a servant before his master,
  for you will be the guilty one
  and a curse will come upon you.
¹¹There is a generation rising that curses their fathers
  and speaks evil of their mothers.
¹²There is a generation rising that considers
    themselves
  to be pure in their own eyes,ᵃ
  yet they are morally filthy,ᵇ unwashed, and unclean.
¹³There is a generation rising that is so filled with
    pride,
  they think they are superior and look down on
    others.

---

a 30:12 See Judg. 21:25.
b 30:12 The Hebrew uses the word *excrement*.

¹⁴There is a generation rising that uses their words like
swords
to cut and slash those who are different.
They would devour the poor, the needy, and the
afflicted
from off the face of the earth!
¹⁵There are three words to describe the greedy:
"Give me more!"
There are some things that are never satisfied.
Forever craving more, they're unable to say, "That's
enough!"
Here are four:
¹⁶the grave, yawning for another victim,
the barren womb, ever wanting a child,
thirsty soil, ever longing for rain,
and a raging fire, devouring its fuel.
They're all insatiable.
¹⁷The eye that mocks his father and dishonors his
elderly mother[a]
deserves to be plucked out by the ravens of the valley
and fed to the young vultures![b]

Four Mysteries

¹⁸There are four marvelous mysteries
that are too amazing to unravel[c]—
who could fully explain them?[d]

---

a 30:17 As translated from the Septuagint.

b 30:17 This is a figure of speech for demonic powers that will remove
their vision. Ravens and vultures are unclean birds associated with
demonic powers in Hebrew poetry.

c 30:18 The Hebrew uses a poetic style of saying there are three mysteries, then saying there are four in order to emphasize their great
importance. There could be within this poetic device a pointing to
the fourth as the key, or the most important.

d 30:18 Notice that each of these four examples have to do with move-
ment and mystery.

¹⁹The way an eagle flies in the sky,[a]
the way a snake glides on a boulder,[b]
the path of a ship as it passes through the sea,[c]
and the way a bridegroom falls in love with his bride.[d]
²⁰Here is the deceptive way of the adulterous woman:[e]
she takes what she wants and then says,
"I've done nothing wrong."

Four Intolerable Things
²¹There are four intolerable events
that[f] are simply unbearable to observe:

---

a 30:19 This is a picture of the overcoming life that soars above its problems and limitations with the wings of an eagle. It could also be a hint of the prophetic revelation that comes to God's servants mysteriously and supernaturally. See Isa. 40:31 and 1 Cor. 2:9–13.

b 30:19 The snake becomes a picture of our sin that was placed on the Rock, Jesus Christ. See Num. 21:6–9; John 3:14–15; 2 Cor. 5:21.

c 30:19 This is a picture of the way our lives, like a ship, sail on the high seas of mystery until we reach our destiny. Our lives contain mysteries, such as where God decided that we were to be born, how we were raised, and the companions who join us until we reach our desired haven. See Ps. 107:23–30.

d 30:19 The Hebrew word translated "bride" can also mean "virgin," pointing to a wedding, thus implying the use of "bridegroom" instead of "man." (Consider Ruth and Boaz.) More important, this is a beautiful metaphor for the mystery of the love of our heavenly Bridegroom (Jesus), who romances his bride and sweeps us off our feet. Love is a mystery. See also 2 Cor. 11:2 and Eph. 5:32.

e 30:20 The adulterous woman of Proverbs is a metaphor for the corrupt religious system. See Rev. 17–18.

f 30:21 See the first footnote for v. 18. These four events each depict a promotion undeserved, a displacing of one who is virtuous with one who is corrupt. Each promotion indicates that they will carry their corruption with them. The unfaithful servant will likely become a tyrant. The fool who becomes wealthy will squander his wealth. The unfaithful woman (or "hated woman") will continue her immorality even after she's married. The girlfriend who replaced the faithful wife will likely find another man one day.

²²when an unfaithful servant becomes a ruler,
  when a scoundrel comes into great wealth,
²³when an unfaithful woman marries a good man,
  and when a mistress replaces a faithful wife.

Four Creatures Small and Wise

²⁴The earth has four creatures that are very small but
  very wise:ᵃ
²⁵The feeble ant has little strength,
  yet look how it diligently gathers its food in the summer
  to last throughout the winter.ᵇ
²⁶The delicate rock-badger isn't all that strong,
  yet look how it makes a secure home, nestled in the
  rocks.ᶜ
²⁷The locusts have no king to lead them,
  yet they cooperate as they move forward by bands.ᵈ
²⁸And the small lizardᵉ is easy to catch
  as it clings to the walls with its hands,
  yet it can be found inside a king's palace.ᶠ

Four Stately Things

²⁹There are four stately monarchsᵍ
  who are impressive to watch as they go forth:

---

a 30:24 Or "They are the epitome of wisdom."
b 30:25 To prepare for the future is a mark of true wisdom.
c 30:26 This becomes a picture of the believer. Though feeling weakness at times, we can make our home in the high place, inside the cleft of the Rock. See John 14:1–3.
d 30:27 The locust army points us to Joel 1–2. There is an awakening army coming to devour the works of the enemy. Their King, though invisible, guides them from on high as one army.
e 30:28 Or "spider."
f 30:28 Though we may see ourselves as insignificant (like the small lizard), God can place us in significant places where we can be used for him.
g 30:29 See the first footnote on v. 18.

³⁰the lion, the king of the jungle, who is afraid of no
one,
³¹the rooster strutting boldly among the hens,ᵃ
the male goat out in front leading the herd,
and a king leading his regal procession.ᵇ
³²If you've acted foolishly by drawing attention to
yourself,
or if you've thought about saying something stupid,
you'd better shut your mouth.
³³For such stupidity may give you a bloody nose!
Stirring up an argument only leads to an angry
confrontation.ᶜ

Inspired Word

31 King Lemuel'sᵈ royal words of wisdom:
These are the inspired words my mother taught
me.ᵉ
²Listen, my dear son, son of my womb.
You are the answer to my prayers, my son.
³So keep yourself sexually pure
from the promiscuous, wayward woman.
Don't waste the strength of your anointing

---

a 30:31 As translated from the Septuagint.

b 30:31 Or "a king surrounded by his band of soldiers." The Hebrew
text is abstruse.

c 30:33 Or "Churning milk makes butter, and punching the nose
brings blood, so stirring up anger produces quarrels." The Hebrew
contains a word play with the word *anger*, which is almost identical
to the word for "nose."

d 31:1 Jewish legend is that King Lemuel was a pseudonym for Solomon, which would make his mother mentioned here to be Bath-
sheba. There is no other mention of Lemuel in the Scriptures. The
Hebrew word translated "inspired words" is *massa*, which some
have surmised was a place, meaning "Lemuel, King of Massa."

e 31:1 The Septuagint is "These are words spoken by God, and through
a king came an answer divine."

    on those who ruin kings—
    you'll live to regret it![a]
⁴For you are a king, Lemuel,
    and it's never fitting for a king to be drunk on wine
    or for rulers to crave alcohol.
⁵For when they drink they forget justice
    and ignore the rights of those in need,
    those who depend on them for leadership.
⁶⁻⁷Strong drink is given to the terminally ill,
    who are suffering at the brink of death.
    Wine is for those in depression
    in order to drown their sorrows.
    Let them drink and forget their poverty and misery.
⁸But you are to be a king who speaks up on behalf
    of the disenfranchised
    and pleads for the legal rights of the defenseless
    and those who are dying.
⁹Be a righteous king, judging on behalf of the poor
    and interceding for those most in need.[b]

The Radiant Bride
    ¹⁰Who could ever find a wife like this one[c]—

---

a 31:3 As translated from the Septuagint.

b 31:9 See James 1:27.

c 31:10 Starting with verse 10 through the end of the book, we have a Hebrew acrostic poem. It is alphabetical in structure, with each of the twenty-two verses beginning with a consecutive letter of the Hebrew alphabet. The implication is that the perfections of this woman would exhaust the entire language. The subject is the perfect bride, the virtuous woman. This woman is both a picture of a virtuous wife and an incredible allegory of the end-time victorious bride of Jesus Christ, full of virtue and grace.

she is a woman of strength and mighty valor!ᵃ
She's full of wealth and wisdom.
The price paid for her was greaterᵇ than many
  jewels.
¹¹Her husband has entrusted his heart to her,ᶜ
for she brings him the rich spoils of victory.
¹²All throughout her life she brings him what is good
  and not evil.ᵈ
¹³She searches out continually to possess
that which is pure and righteous.ᵉ

---

a 31:10 The Hebrew word used to describe this virtuous wife is *khayil*. The meaning of this word cannot be contained by one English equivalent word. It is often used in connection with military prowess. This is a warring wife. *Khayil* can be translated "mighty;" "wealthy;" "excellent;" "morally righteous;" "full of substance, integrity, abilities, and strength;" "mighty like an army." The wife is a metaphor for the last-days church, the virtuous, overcoming bride of Jesus Christ. The word *khayil* is most often used to describe valiant men. See Ex. 18:21, where it is used for the mighty ones Moses was to commission as elders and leaders among the people. Because many of the cultural terms and metaphors used in this passage are not understood or even used in today's English-speaking world, this translation makes them explicit.

b 31:10 Or "her worth." The price paid for her was the sacred blood of the Lamb of God, her Bridegroom.

c 31:11 Or "has great confidence in her."

d 31:12 The virtuous bride will not bring disgrace to his name. Jesus will not be ashamed to display her to the world.

e 31:13 Or "wool and linen [flax]." Wool is a metaphor often used as a symbol of what is pure. See Isa. 1:18; Dan. 7:9; Rev. 1:14. Linen was made from flax and always speaks of righteousness. The priests of the Old Testament wore linen garments as they went before God's presence to offer sacrifices. The curtains of the tabernacle were likewise made of linen, signifying God's righteousness. See Ex. 28:39–43 and Rev. 19:8. The virtuous bride of Christ in the last days will be seeking for only what is pure and righteous in the eyes of her Bridegroom.

She delights in the work of her hands.[a]
[14]She gives out revelation-truth[b] to feed others.
She is like a trading ship bringing divine supplies[c]
from the merchant.[d]
[15]Even in the night season[e] she arises[f] and sets food on
the table
for hungry ones in her house and for others.[g]
[16]She sets her heart upon a field[h] and takes it as her
own.

---

a 31:13 Or "eagerly works with her hands." The hands, with their five
fingers, speak of the five ministries of the present work of Christ
on the earth: apostles, prophets, evangelists, pastors, and teachers.
These are often referred to as the five-fold ministries. Her delight is
to equip others and help those in need.

b 31:14 Or "bread." This is a consistent emblem of spiritual food.

c 31:14 Or "supplies from far away." The implication is that the supplies come from another realm. She is bringing heavenly manna for
those she feeds.

d 31:14 Or "like merchant ships bringing goods." Like a ship loaded
with cargo, the bride of Christ brings heavenly treasures to others.
The use of the term *merchant* points to Jesus Christ. He is described
as a merchant in Matt. 13:45 in the parable of the extraordinary
pearl. The "pearl" is the church or the believer, which cost all that
Jesus had (his blood) to purchase us.

e 31:15 She is interceding in the night, laboring in a night season to
help others.

f 31:15 The Hebrew word translated "arise" can also mean "to rise
up in power." We are told to "rise up in splendor and be radiant, for
your light has dawned" in Isa. 60:1, which uses the same Hebrew
word for "arise." The bride of Christ will arise with anointing to feed
and bless the people of God.

g 31:15 Or "female servants." The servants are a metaphor for other
churches and ministries.

h 31:16 Or "a land" or "a country."

She labors there to plant the living vines.*

¹⁷She wraps herself in strength,* might, and power in
all her works.

¹⁸She tastes and experiences a better substance,*
and her shining light will not be extinguished,
no matter how dark the night.*

¹⁹She stretches out her hands to help the needy*
and she lays hold of the wheels of government.*

²⁰She is known by her extravagant generosity to the poor,
for she always reaches out her hands* to those in need.

²¹She is not afraid of tribulation,*
for all her household is covered in the dual garments*

---

a 31:16 Or "By the fruit of her hands she plants a vineyard." (The
Septuagint is "possession.") For "hands," see the second footnote
for v. 13. This vineyard becomes a metaphor for the local church.
We are the branches of the Vine (Christ). See John 15:1–8. She is
passionate about bringing forth fruit. She becomes a missionary to
the nations, planting churches and bringing new life.

b 31:17 Or "She girds her loins with strength and makes her shoulders
strong." This is a figure of speech for being anointed with power to
do the works of Jesus. See John 14:12.

c 31:18 Or "good merchandise."

d 31:18 Her prayer life ("light") overcomes her circumstances, even in
a culture where darkness prevails.

e 31:19 As translated from the Septuagint. The Hebrew uses a term
for "distaff" (a weaver's staff), which is taken from a root word for
"prosperity." The poetic nuance of this phrase is that she uses her
prosperity to bless the needy.

f 31:19 Or "Her hands grasp the spindle." The word translated as
"spindle" can also mean "governmental circuits" or "wheels." There
is a hint here of the wheels mentioned in Ezek. 1. The throne of
God's government sits on flaming wheels. See Dan. 7:9.

g 31:20 Notice the mention of her hands. See the second footnote for v. 13.

h 31:21 Or "snow." This is a figure of speech for the fear of a cold
winter season.

i 31:21 As translated from the Septuagint. The Hebrew is "everyone is
covered in scarlet [blood]." Grace has brought righteousness to those
in her house (under her ministry).

of righteousness and grace.
[22]Her clothing is beautifully knit together[a]—
a purple gown of exquisite linen.
[23]Her husband is famous and admired by all,
sitting as the venerable judge of his people.[b]
[24]Even her works of righteousness[c]
she does[d] for the benefit of her enemies.[e]
[25]Bold power and glorious majesty[f] are wrapped
around her
as she laughs with joy over the latter days.[g]
[26]Her teachings are filled with wisdom and kindness
as loving instruction pours from her lips.[h]
[27]She watches over the ways of her household[i]
and meets every need they have.

---

a 31:22 This clothing speaks of the ministries of the body of Christ,
woven and knit together by the Holy Spirit. See Eph. 4:15–16 and
Col. 2:2.

b 31:23 Or "sitting at the city gates among the elders of the land."
Judgment was rendered at the gates of a city in that day. It was their
courtroom. Our heavenly King is also the Judge. So famous, so glorious, yet he is our Bridegroom.

c 31:24 Or "linen." See the second footnote for v. 13 regarding linen
as a symbol for righteousness.

d 31:24 Or "sells them." The root word for "sell" can also mean
"surrender."

e 31:24 Or "aprons or belts for the Canaanites." The Canaanites were
the traditional enemies of the Hebrews.

f 31:25 Or "Beauty, honor, and excellence."

g 31:25 The virtuous and victorious bride has no fear for the days
to come. She contemplates eternity and her forever union with the
Bridegroom.

h 31:26 The Septuagint is "she opens her mouth carefully and
lawfully."

i 31:27 Or "She is a watchman over her house [family]."

²⁸Her sons and daughters arise*ᵃ* in one accord to extol
her virtues,*ᵇ*
and her husband arises to speak of her in glowing
terms.*ᶜ*
²⁹"There are many valiant and noble ones,*ᵈ*
but you have ascended above them all!"*ᵉ*
³⁰Charm can be misleading,
and beauty is vain and so quickly fades,
but this virtuous woman lives in the wonder, awe,
and fear of the Lord.
She will be praised *throughout eternity.*
³¹So go ahead and give her the credit that is due,
for she has become a radiant woman,
and all her loving works of righteousness deserve to
be admired
at the gateways of every city!*ᶠ*

---

a 31:28 The Hebrew word translated "arise" can also mean "to rise up
with power." The Septuagint is "She raises her children so they will
grow rich."

b 31:28 Or "Hooray, hooray for our mother!"

c 31:28 For more of how the heavenly Bridegroom loves his bride,
read the Song of Songs.

d 31:29 Or "Many daughters have obtained wealth because of her."
These valiant and noble ones (daughters) represent the church
of previous generations who remained faithful in their pursuit of
Jesus. But this final generation will be the bridal company of the
lovers of God who do mighty exploits and miracles on the earth.

e 31:29 Or "you are first in his eyes." See Song. 6:8–9.

f 31:31 The Septuagint could be translated "her husband is praised at
the city gates."

YOUR PERSONAL INVITATION

TO FOLLOW JESUS

We can all find ourselves in dark places needing some light—light that brings direction, healing, vision, warmth, and hope. Jesus said, "I am light to the world, and those who embrace me will experience life-giving light, and they will never walk in darkness" (John 8:12). Without the light and love of Jesus, this world is truly a dark place and we are lost forever.

Love unlocks mysteries. As we love Jesus, our hearts are unlocked to see more of his beauty and glory. When we stop defining ourselves by our failures, but rather as the ones whom Jesus loves, our hearts begin to open to the breathtaking discovery of the wonder of Jesus Christ.

All that is recorded in the Scriptures is there so that you will fully believe that Jesus is the Son of God, and that through your faith in him you will experience eternal life by the power of his name (see John 20:31).

If you want this light and love in your life, say a prayer like this—whether for the first time or to express again your passionate desire to follow Jesus:

Jesus, you are the light of the world. I want to follow you, passionately and wholeheartedly. But my sins have separated me from you. Thank you for your love for me. Thank you for paying the price for my sins. I trust your finished work on the cross for my rescue. I turn away from the thoughts and deeds that have separated me from you. Forgive me and awaken me to love you with all my heart, mind, soul, and strength. I believe God raised you from the dead, and I want that new life to flow through me each day and for eternity. God, I give you my life. Fill me with your Spirit so that my life will honor you and I can fulfill your purpose for me. Amen.

You can be assured that what Jesus said about those who choose to follow him is true: "If you embrace my message and believe in the One who sent me, you will never face condemnation, for in me, you have already passed from the realm of death into the realm of eternal life!" (John 5:24). But there's more! Not only are you declared "not guilty" by God because of Jesus, you are also considered his most intimate friend (John 15:15).

As you grow in your relationship with Jesus, continue to read the Bible, communicate with God through prayer, spend time with others who follow Jesus, and live out your faith daily and passionately. God bless you!

ABOUT THE
TRANSLATOR

Brian Simmons is known as a passionate lover of God. After a dramatic conversion to Christ, Brian knew that God was calling him to go to the unreached people of the world and present the gospel of God's grace to all who would listen. With his wife, Candice, and their three children, he spent nearly eight years in the tropical rain forest of the Darien Province of Panama as a church planter, translator, and consultant. Having been trained in linguistics and Bible translation principles, Brian assisted in the Paya-Kuna New Testament translation project, and after their ministry in the jungle, Brian was instrumental in planting a thriving church in New England (U.S.). He is the lead translator for The Passion Translation Project and travels full time as a speaker and Bible teacher. He has been happily married to Candice since 1971 and boasts regularly of his three children and eight grandchildren.

Follow The Passion Translation at:

Facebook.com/passiontranslation
Twitter.com/tPtBible
Instagram.com/passiontranslation

For more information about the translation project please visit:

ThePassionTranslation.com

Encounter the Heart of God

The Passion Translation is a modern, easy-to-read Bible translation that unlocks the passion of God's heart and expresses his fiery love—merging emotion and life-changing truth. This translation will evoke an overwhelming response in every reader, unfolding the deep mysteries of Scripture. If you are hungry for God, The Passion Translation will help you encounter his heart and know him more intimately. Fall in love with God all over again.

The Passion Translation®
The New Testament with Psalms, Proverbs, and Song of Songs
2020 Edition

Available in a variety of styles, including pearlescent hardcover, faux leather, fabric hardcover, standard, compact, and large print.

NEW FEATURES

- Over 1000 new and revised in-depth footnotes with insightful study notes, commentary, word studies, cross references, and alternate translations
- Updated text
- 16 pages of full-color maps

STANDARD FEATURES

- Extensive introductions
- Contemporary font in traditional two-column format
- Premium Bible paper stitched together with layflat Smyth-sewn binding
- Ribbon marker

THE
PASSION
TRANSLATION

ThePassionTranslation.com

The Passion Translation®
The New Testament with Psalms, Proverbs, and Song of Songs
2020 Edition

STANDARD HARDCOVER

Ivory

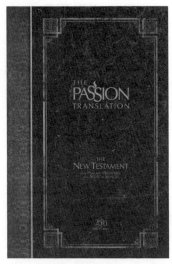

Espresso

Peony

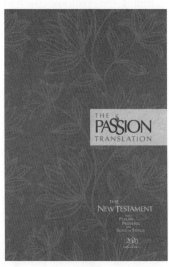

Floral

The Passion Translation®
The New Testament with Psalms, Proverbs, and Song of Songs
2020 Edition

STANDARD FAUX LEATHER

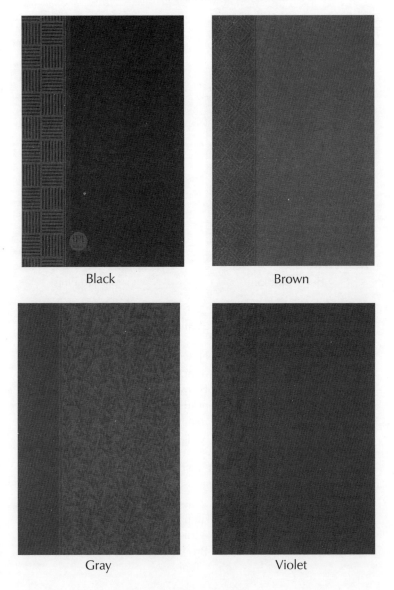

Black

Brown

Gray

Violet

The Passion Translation®
The New Testament with Psalms, Proverbs, and Song of Songs
2020 Edition

STANDARD FABRIC HARDCOVER

Berry Blossom   Passion in Plum

Also available in

LARGE PRINT FAUX LEATHER
Black
Brown
Burgundy
Navy
Violet

COMPACT FAUX LEATHER
Charcoal
Navy
Fuchsia
Violet
Brown
Teal

ThePassionTranslation.com

NOTES

THE PASSION
TRANSLATION

ThePassionTranslation.com